W9-AVL-805

COLOSSAL CARTOONING

Over 750 Ways to Tell Your Story

STERLING INNOVATION

An imprint of Sterling Publishing Co., Inc.

New York / London
www.sterlingpublishing.com

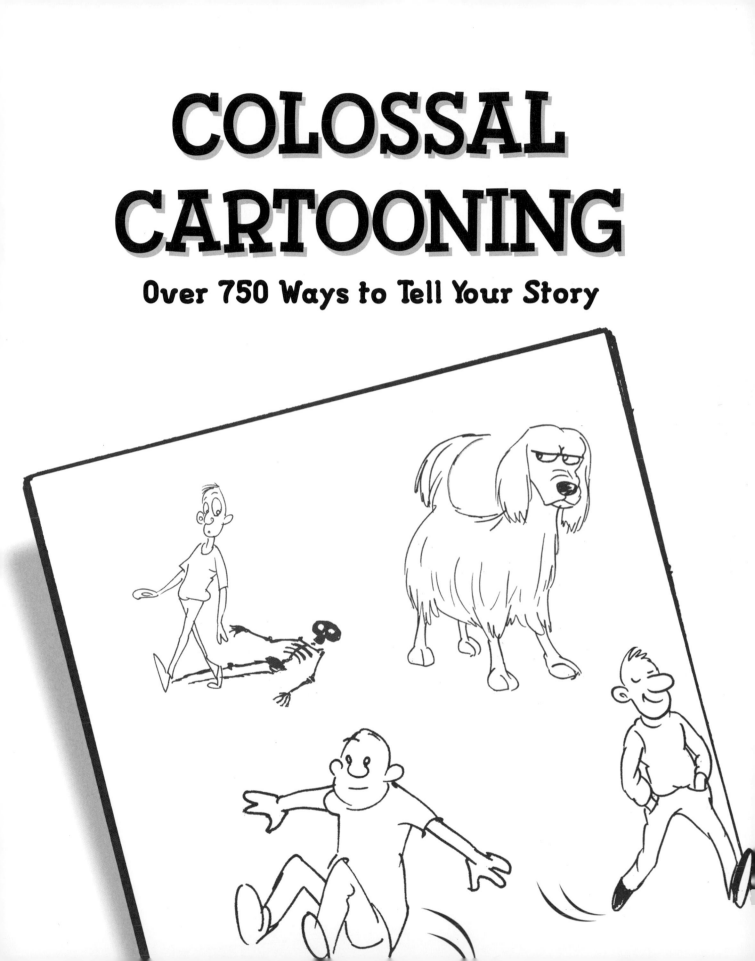

COLOSSAL CARTOONING

Over 750 Ways to Tell Your Story

STERLING, the Sterling logo, STERLING INNOVATION, and the Sterling Innovation logo
are registered trademarks of Sterling Publishing Co., Inc.

10 9 8 7 6 5 4 3 2 1

Published by Sterling Publishing Co., Inc.
387 Park Avenue South, New York, NY 10016
© 2009 by Sterling Publishing Co., Inc.

Distributed in Canada by Sterling Publishing
C/o Canadian Manda Group, 165 Dufferin Street
Toronto, Ontario, Canada M6K 3H6
Distributed in the United Kingdom by GMC Distribution Services
Castle Place, 166 High Street, Lewes, East Sussex, England BN7 1XU
Distributed in Australia by Capricorn Link (Australia) Pty. Ltd.
P.O. Box 704, Windsor, NSW 2756, Australia

Content, Design, and Illustrations by

quadrum■
Content Services. Powered by design!

www.quadrumltd.com

Cover design by Bonnie Naugle

Images on page 180 and 181 used under license from Shutterstock.com

Printed in Singapore
All rights reserved

Sterling ISBN 978-1-4027-6528-5

For information about custom editions, special sales, premium and
corporate purchases, please contact Sterling Special Sales
Department at 800-805-5489 or specialsales@sterlingpublishing.com.

Contents

Contents

Chapter 1

What Makes an Illustration Funny?

Faces

There are several things that can make an illustration funny. Facial expressions, drawing technique, and comic timing are important parts to making your drawings funny. Let's work on mastering faces first.

When someone is talking, you instinctively notice their facial expressions and their hand movements. The way they roll their eyes, stick out their tongue, look skyward, or scowl—it is the expressions that set the first mood for a visual.

Expressions are one of the easiest things to draw. Here's how:

First, draw a circle for the head. Make two small circles on the sides for ears, then add the eyes—**circles or dots for open eyes** and **horizontal lines or Vs for closed eyes**. Next, draw an extended loop for the nose. And finally, fill in **semicircles for cheeks** and **curves for a grin** (as shown below). And you're on your way!

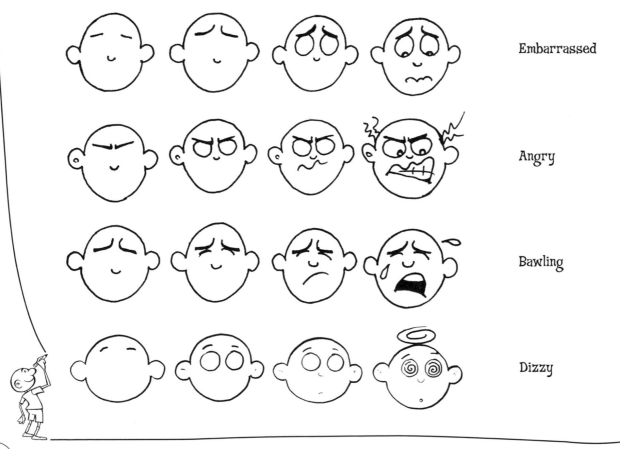

Embarrassed

Angry

Bawling

Dizzy

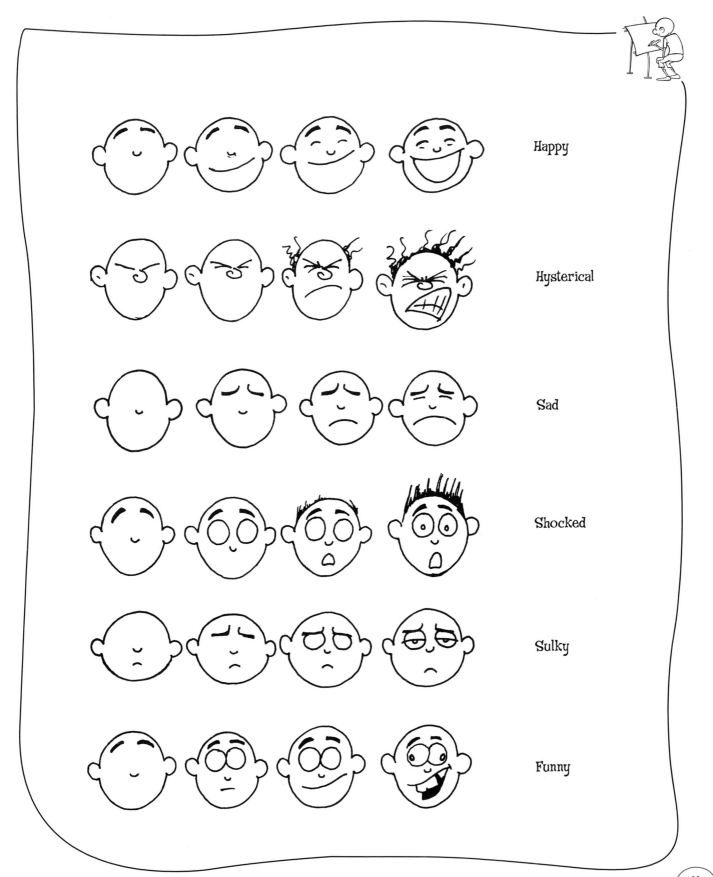

Happy

Hysterical

Sad

Shocked

Sulky

Funny

Exaggeration

Cartooning isn't only about expressions. When cartooning, you can take a lot of liberties and use the art of exaggeration as well. All you have to do is change the proportions, shapes, and sizes of different body parts.

For instance, you can **enlarge the head, lengthen the arms and legs, use round or square bellies, big ears or eyes, large hands and feet,** and **droopy shoulders.**

Practice—don't be afraid to experiment. You'll get the hang of it. Every bit of exaggeration adds personality to the character you are creating.

Big ears

Big eyes

Long nose

Oversized body

Oversized head

Long, long legs

Extra-long arms

Drawing Technique

Ever wondered how using different strokes can define the style of cartoon?

You can use **straight lines, curves, dots,** or **strokes** to add interesting elements. Sometimes a deft stroke can convey in an instant what an entire sentence would say in words.

Curved lines flow smoothly into one another.

Join the dots to make the figure.

Straight lines give the cartoon an edgy look.

Smooth strokes, incomplete in themselves, create the total picture.

Comic Timing

Proceed to the next level and practice the art of comic timing. This technique is usually used when there is a series of drawings. One of these drawings, usually the last, is called a **visual punch line**.

Doodle Page

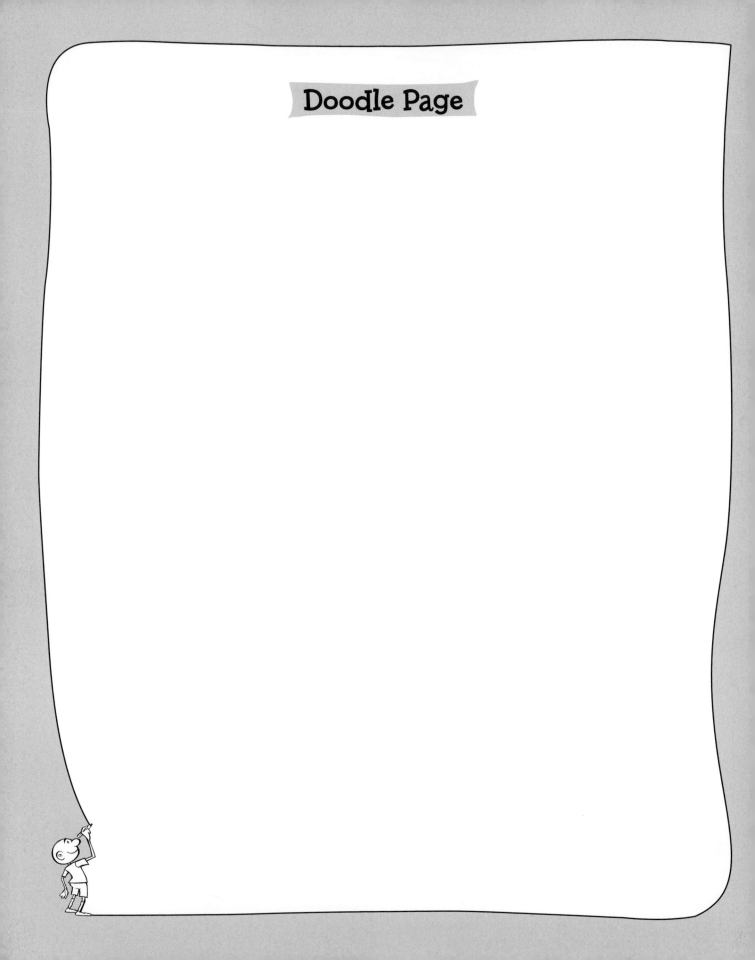

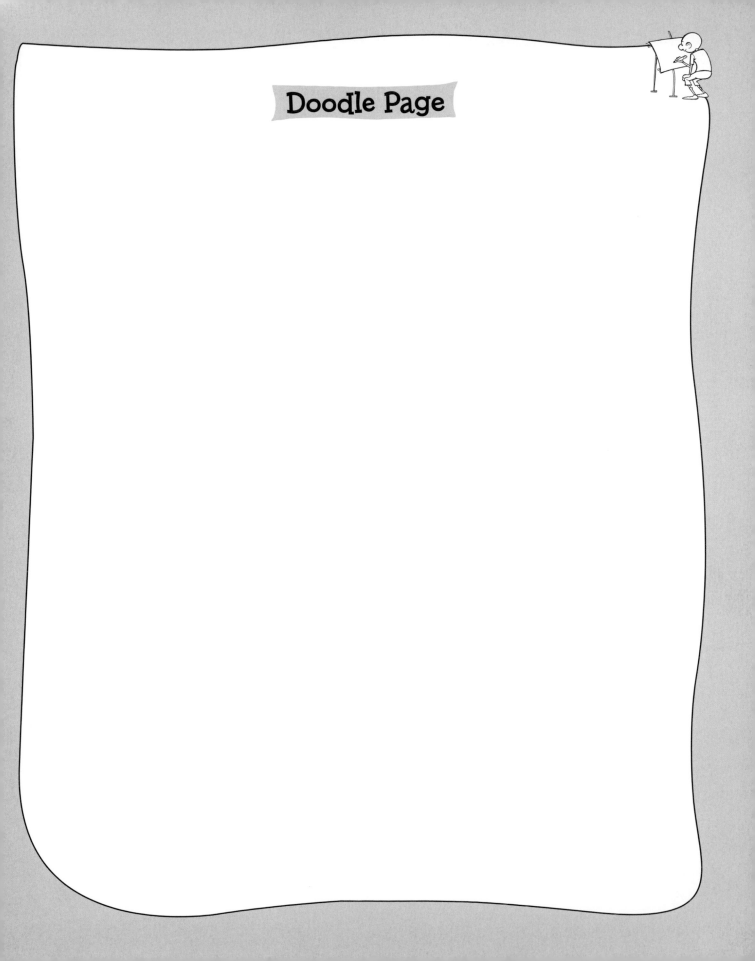

Doodle Page

Chapter 2

Doodling Basics

Chapter 2

Shapes

Before you pick up your pencil, think of different **shapes**. You can use basic shapes to draw different characters. And here's a tip—try not to draw over the same shape several times. Try to get it right the first time. Look at the examples below and see how any shape can be the basis for a facial structure.

Basic Sketches

Now extend your imagination and allow your pencil to doodle away and create basic sketches of your character in action.

Tools

Getting it right means picking the right drawing tool—**pencil, pen, marker, brush, charcoal**, etc. Each tool lends a different look to your cartoon. You could first sketch with a pencil and then ink in the lines. Or, if you're feeling adventurous, draw directly with the tool of your choice!

Take a look at the effects that different tools can have on your drawings.

Pencil

Fountain pen

Sketch pen

Marker

Charcoal

Point brush

Texture

What's a drawing without texture? You can use different kinds of paper or even an illustration board to lend texture to your cartoon.

For instance, there are **smooth paper**, **handmade paper**, and **textured paper**.

Textured paper gives the outlines of your sketch a jagged effect, adding interest.

Heavy, quality drawing paper is smooth and allows your sketch to breathe on its own.

Handmade paper will give your sketch depth and dimension.

Doodle Page

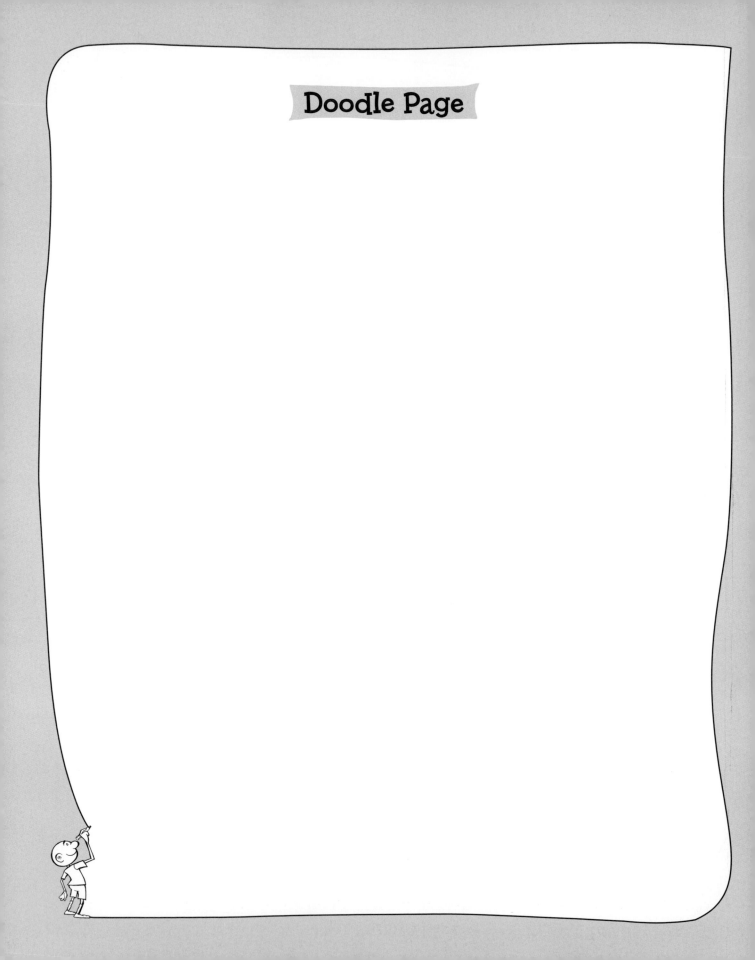

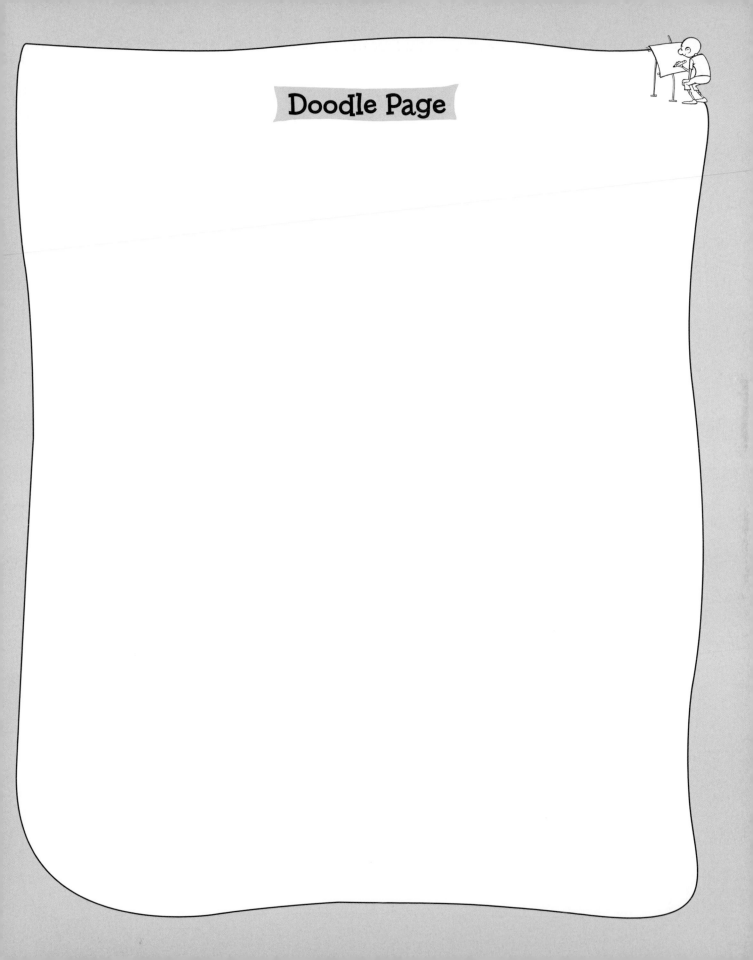

Doodle Page

Chapter 3

Drawing
a Character

What you see isn't always what you get!!!

Chapter 3

Characteristics

Drawing characters is a lot of fun and they can be inspired by everyday people—**the mailman, the boss, the gossip next door, or the cute little girl who visits the neighbors.**

But, as in real life, people are most interesting when they have unique characteristics. So how do you give each one a distinct characteristic?

Here are some characteristics you can draw from:

Optimist

Pessimist

Tough guy

Crooked

Nasty

Gossip

Arrogant

Depressive

Mischief maker

Goofy

Academic

Easygoing

Underdog

Fashionable

Punk

Flirt

Expressions

Facial expressions are a dead giveaway of a person's thoughts and feelings. All you have to do is get the expression right, then exaggerate it.

Take the eyes, nose, and mouth of your character and play around with them. The way each of these is drawn defines your character's personality. Eyebrows also add to the expression. For example, **the angry guy has thin eyebrows that bend in a V shape, the cunning guy has a wide, toothy grin,** and so on.

Annoyed	Resigned	Confused	Sly
Laughing	Surprised	Amused	Angry
Concentrating	Confident	Tragic	Cunning

Remember, it's all about using the right combination of eyes, nose, and mouth. Let's see what you can create by using different combinations.

Sulky

Horrified

Funny

Guilty

Doleful

Hungry

Tickled pink

Listening

Suspicious

Scared

Shocked

Shy

Clueless

Coy

Dreamy

Naughty

Mournful

Embarrassed

Dizzy

Zonked

Exasperated

Happy

In pain

Smug

Tired

Furious

Bored

Calm

Curious

Weepy

Stoic

Aghast

Posture

The way a person stands, sits, or walks—his or her posture—betrays a mood or an emotion, too. Look at the following examples:

Haven't a clue.

I'm thinking.

Out!!

Hmmm . . .

I did it!!

Here I am!

Ahhh, time to relax!

Personalities

All of your characters should have a distinct personality, and it's up to you to give it to them using the characteristics, expressions, and postures discussed in this chapter.

For example, **the bully** might have small, squinted eyes, thin, elongated legs, and a large, overexaggerated upper body; **the boss** might have a rounded body with prominent lips, and his head might be bent forward slightly.

The Boss

The Gossip

The Bully

The Defeated

The Nag

The Neighbor

The Shy Guy

The Cynic

The Flirt

39

Actions

People who don't do anything can be boring people. The same is true for cartoon characters.

What would you like your character to do? Drawing actions is both fun and challenging. Make your character do all sorts of things, from running to falling down.

Falling down

Hitting

Kicking

Jumping

Running

Throwing

How Old Are They?

What is your character saying without really saying it? The personality of your character is shaped by subtle details. For instance, age can be indicated by **hair, spectacles, clothing,** and **even the way your character sits or stands**.

Simple characteristics define the age of your character.

Middle-aged

Teenager

Kid

Baby

Early 30s

Elderly

Body Language

Personality traits are also communicated through **body language**. Take a look at these examples:

Aggressive

Diffident

Happy-go-lucky

Sly

Character Sheet

Now that you have decided on your character's personality, it helps to take stock. Character designers use **character sheets** to show how the character looks from different angles. This is especially useful for animators, and it ensures continuity of the character in the frames.

Front view

Profile view

Three-quarter view

In action

Doodle Page

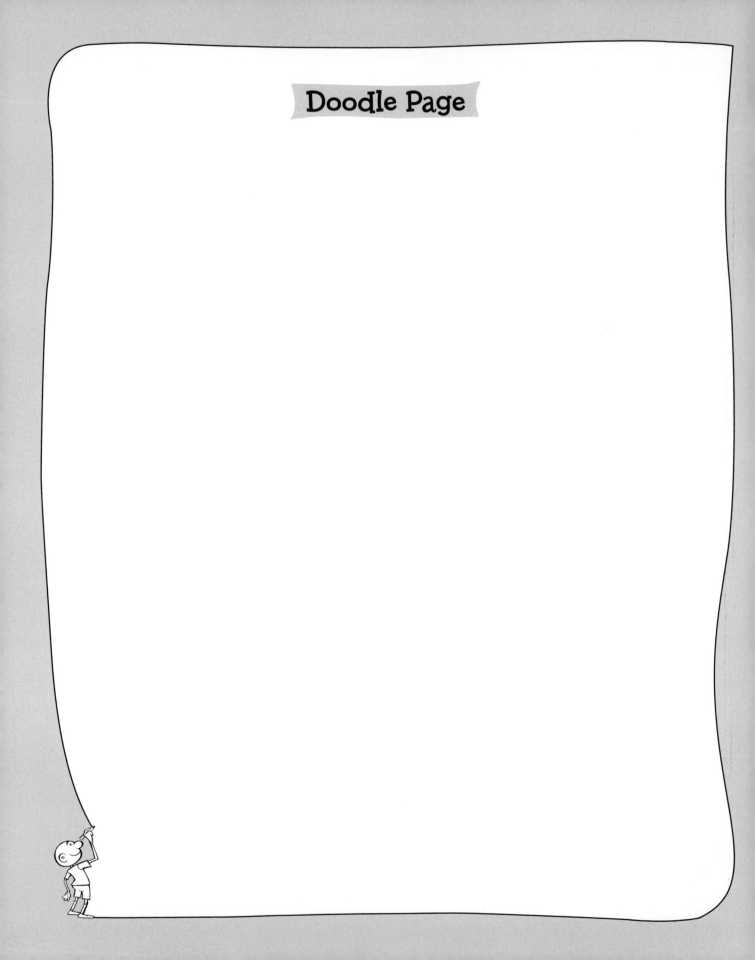

Doodle Page

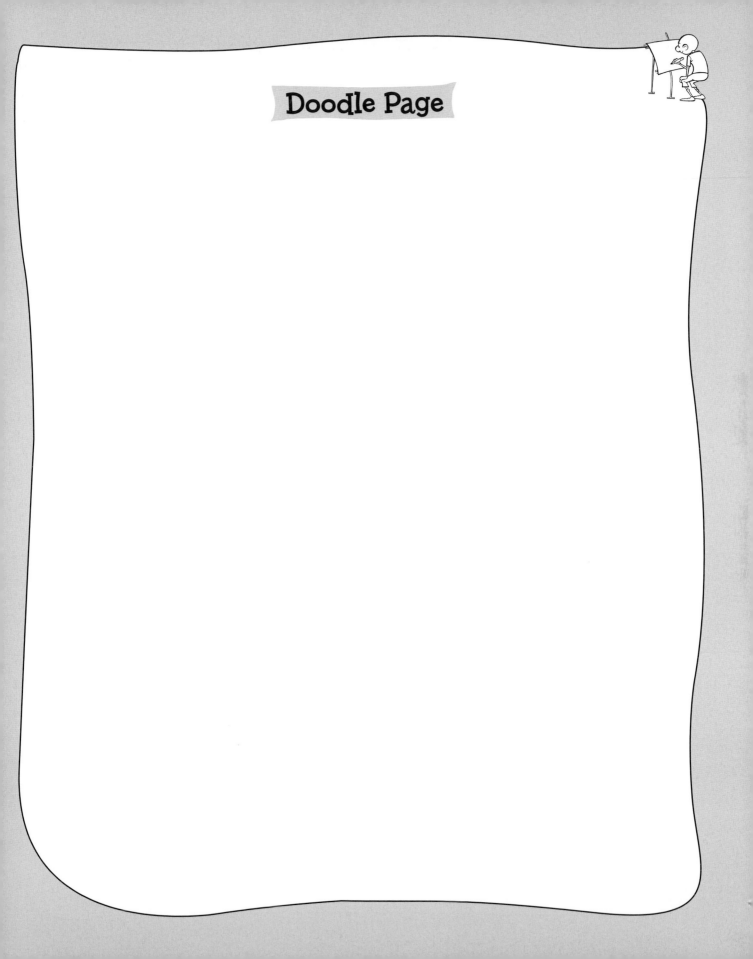

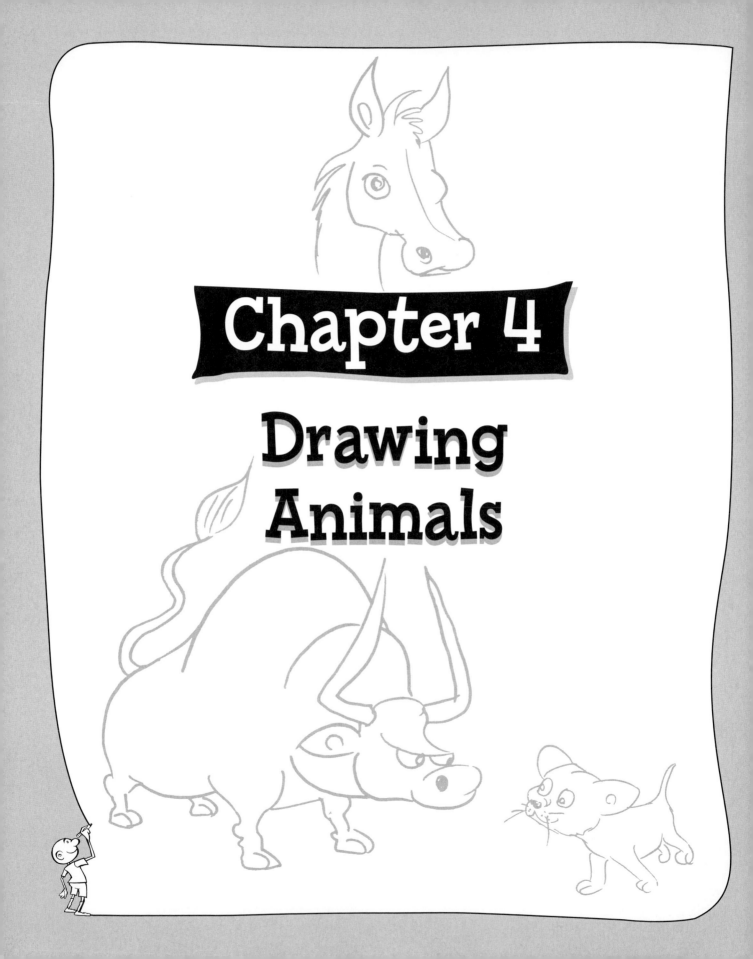

Chapter 4

Drawing Animals

Chapter 4

Introduction

Drawing animals can be both fun and challenging. In this chapter you'll find instructions and helpful tips for drawing animals, as well as step-by-step directions for creating specific animals such as dogs and cats.

The challenge is to capture unique features in your drawing, and then add the appropriate expression.

It is often helpful to simplify the body structure by breaking it down into:

1. the head and neck   2. the belly   3. the rear

It is a good idea to think of each body section in terms of shapes, such as circles, ovals, cylinders, and squares.

Some Tips for Drawing Animals

*   When drawing the head, divide the skull into three basic parts: the muzzle, the nose, and the skull.

*   When drawn in profile, the nose, eye, and ear of animals often line up.

*   Except for cats, dogs, and bears, the eyes are normally placed on the sides of the head.

*   Imagine the body of an animal like a rubber ball, and don't forget to keep in mind one of the basic rules of animation—SQUASH and STRETCH!

Use the steps below to draw a **cat**:

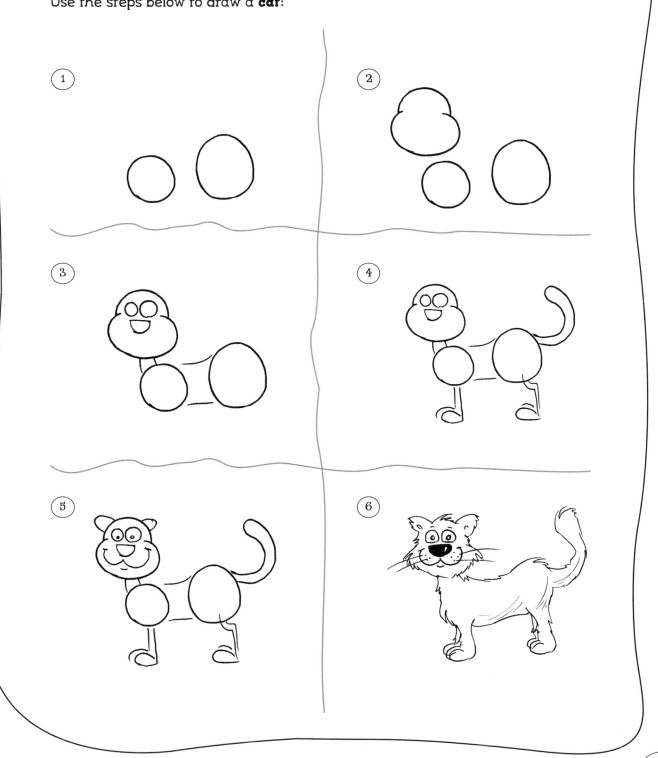

Chapter 4

Here's how to draw a **dog**:

Here's how to draw a **cow**:

Chapter 4

Here's how to draw an **elephant**:

1
2
3
4
5
6

52

Here's how to draw a **parrot**:

Chapter 4

Here's how to draw a **pig**:

① ② ③ ④ ⑤ ⑥

Here's how to draw a **tiger**:

Here are examples of animals in different poses:

Doodle Page

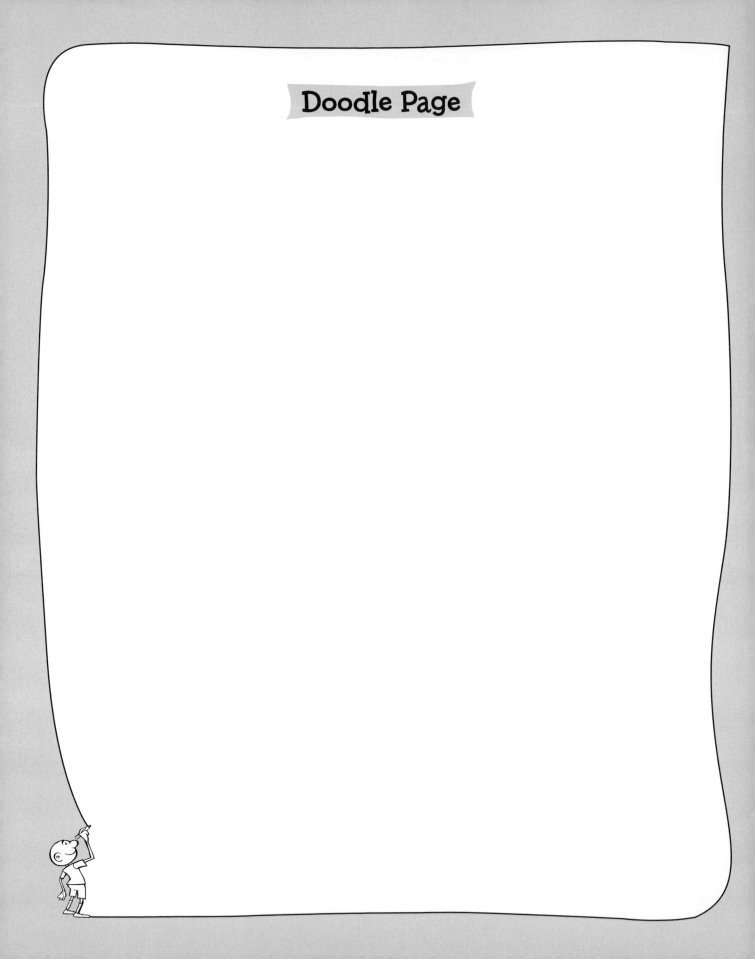

Chapter 5

Special Effects

WHEEEE!!!

Chapter 5

Movement Lines

Even the most carefully sketched cartoon figure has something missing if it doesn't include special effects. Special effects add depth to your drawing and a dimension that brings out its essence.

There are many standard effects but once you get the hang of them, you can make up your own!

Movement Lines are lines that suggest movement in an action drawing. Just a couple of **horizontal, vertical,** or **curved lines** and you're on your way!

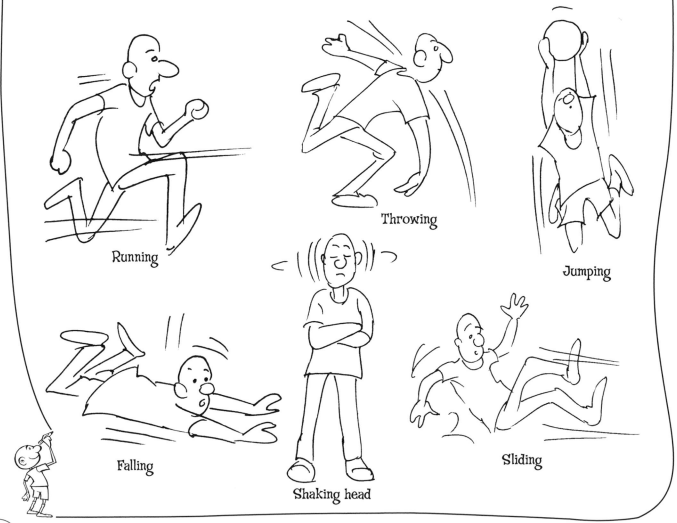

Running

Throwing

Jumping

Falling

Shaking head

Sliding

Stars, Planets, Puff Clouds, Bubbles

Stars, planets, puff clouds, and **thought bubbles** are some special effects you can use to add more depth and entertainment to your illustrations. **Puff clouds** can be used to show speed; **bubbles** suggest breathing underwater; **Stars** and **planets** can show confusion; **thought bubbles,** can "speak" your character's mind.

Here are some examples:

Baffled

Underwater

Dreamy

Aggression

Dizzy

Fleeing

Other Special Effects

Slapping

Anger

Deep sleep

Speeding off

Kicked out

Stinky

Shadows

A shadow is not just something that follows you in the dark; shadows can be used to add depth or to make a gag!

Shadows can also be used to inject drama into a cartoon. They are particularly effective in night scenes. You can add shadows to the characters as well as to surroundings and background, such as buildings and trees.

Shadows are also used extensively in superhero comics and graphic novels, to build atmosphere as required by the story line.

Doodle Page

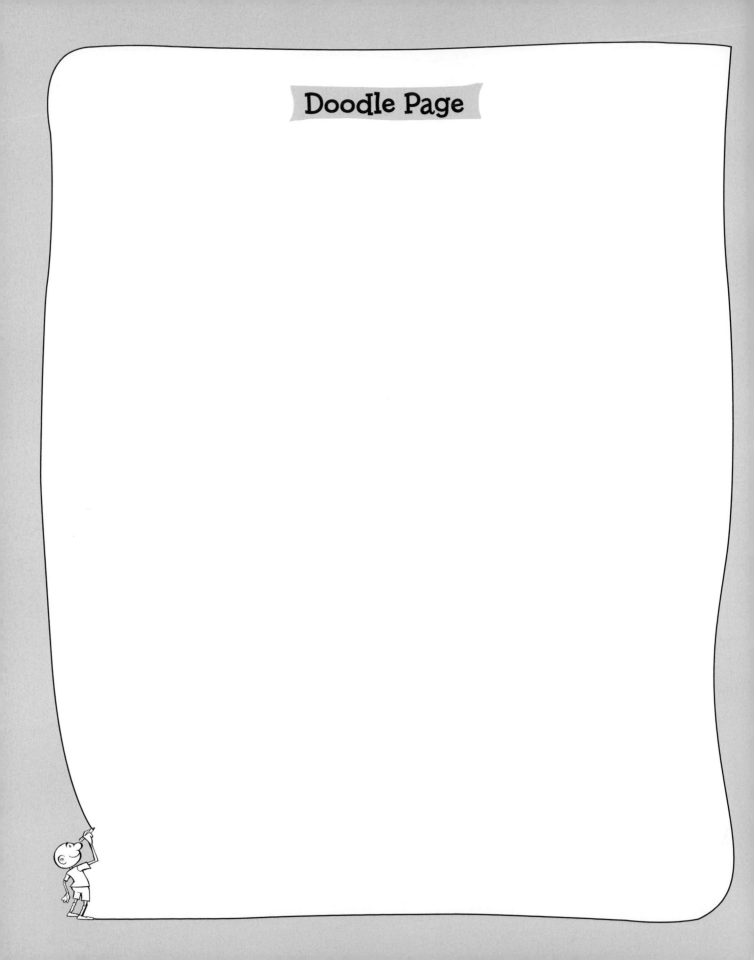

Doodle Page

Chapter 6

Cartoon Language

Chapter 6

Sound Words

How often have you "heard" a cartoon go **biff**!, **bam**! or **boom**!? These are dramatic **sound words** which reinforce certain actions and are usually used in comic art. But remember, use only universal expressions, ones which readers remember and recognize because they are often used.

Try these:

And still more:

Cartoon Language

And still more:

Blurbs

Who says a good drawing says it all? Add a speech bubble and it could say much more!

There are different kinds of **speech bubbles** or **blurbs,** depending on what your character is saying and how he or she is saying it.

Notice the choice of speech bubble:

Talking–simple speech bubble

Thinking or dreaming–thought bubble

Talking loudly–spiky speech bubble

Exclamation marks and question marks

And here's how they can be used. Notice the last has no bubble at all but still has impact.

Sounds

Some sounds have a "look" attached. And some looks have a "sound" attached. Here are some examples of both.

Doodle Page

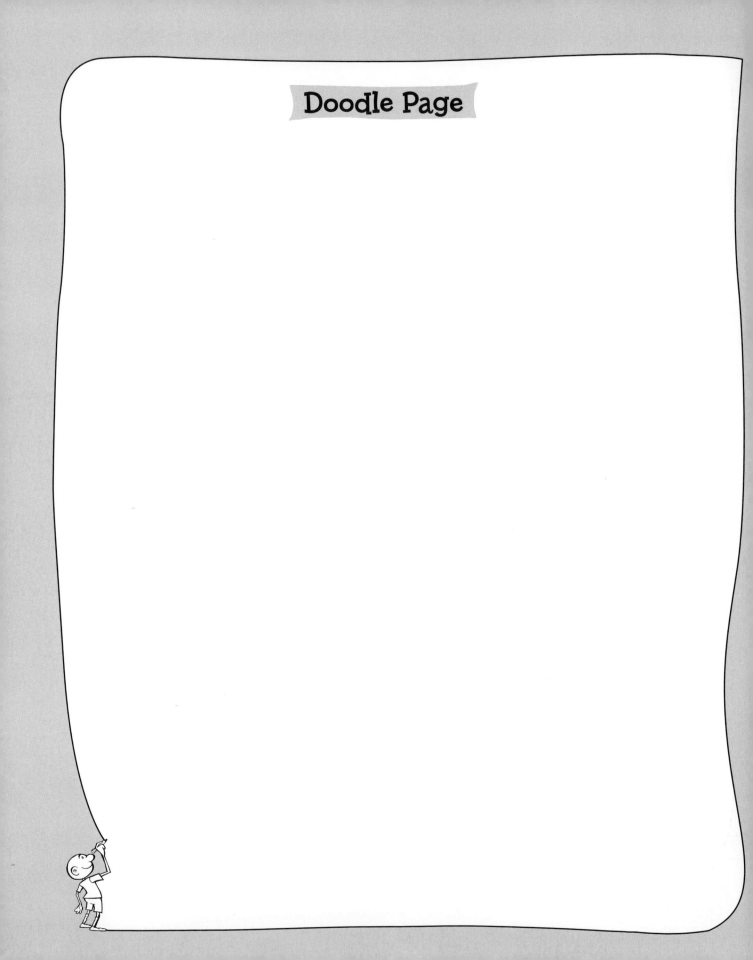

Doodle Page

Chapter 7

Basic Anatomy

Ack!! Is that the inside of me!?!

Going Realistic

If you're inclined to draw realistic cartoons, like the ones in superhero comics, a lesson in basic anatomy is a must. First, draw the **basic body structure**, using the joints to determine the proportion of the limbs. Then define the figure with basic shapes and detail it.

Making "Head" Way

Here are some positions of the head. Observe the angles and how they show movement.

Upward

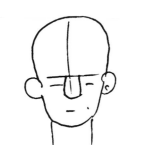  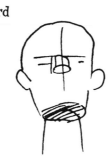 

Downward

To the left

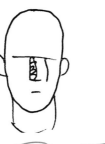

To the right and tilted

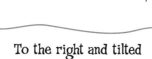

Hands-on

Here are some positions of hands in preliminary strokes before detail is added:

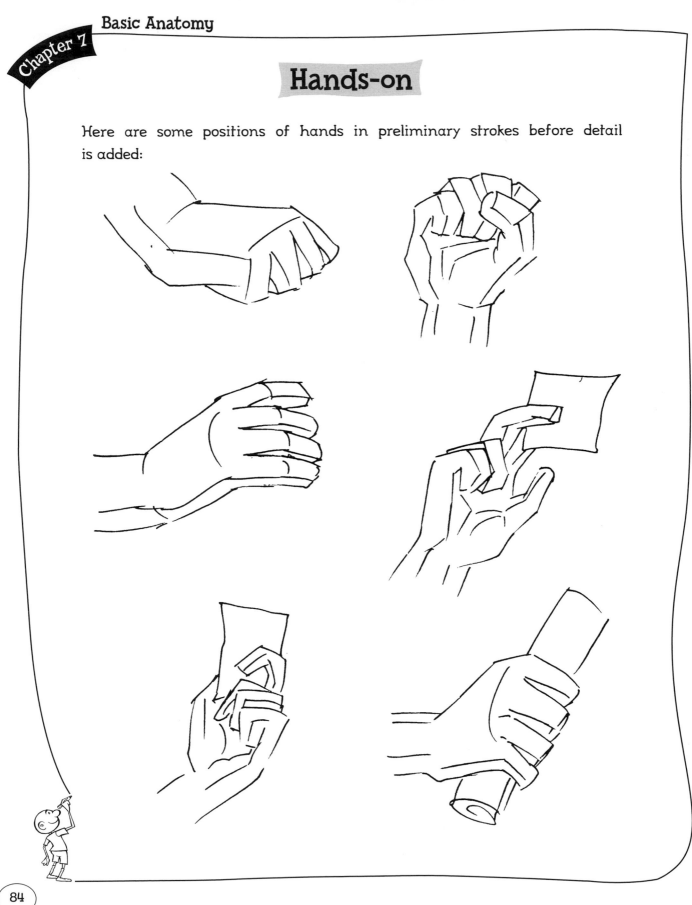

And with some hand detail added:

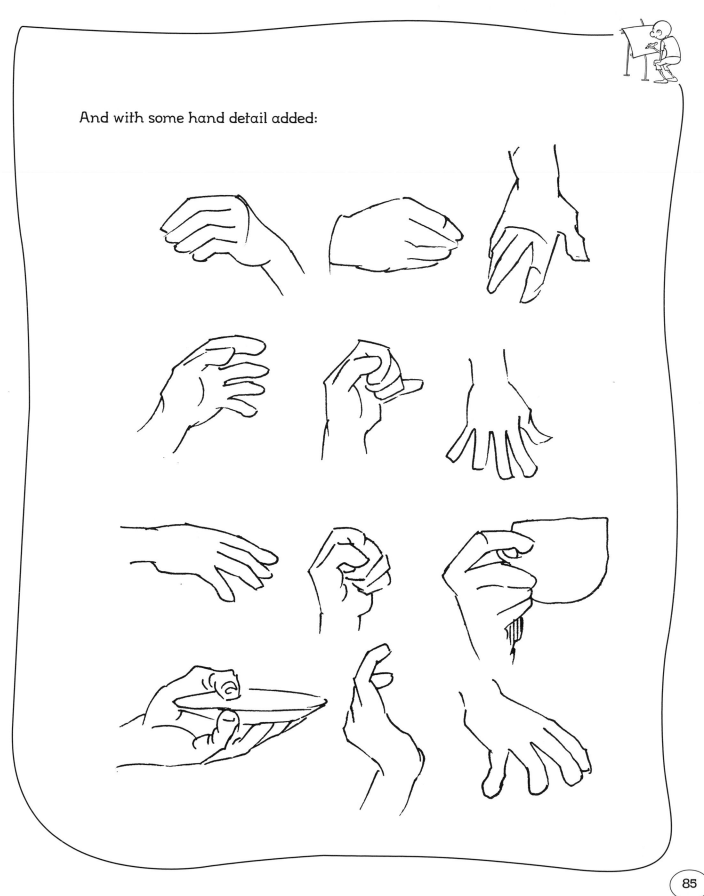

Playing Footsie

Here are some positions of feet before detail is added:

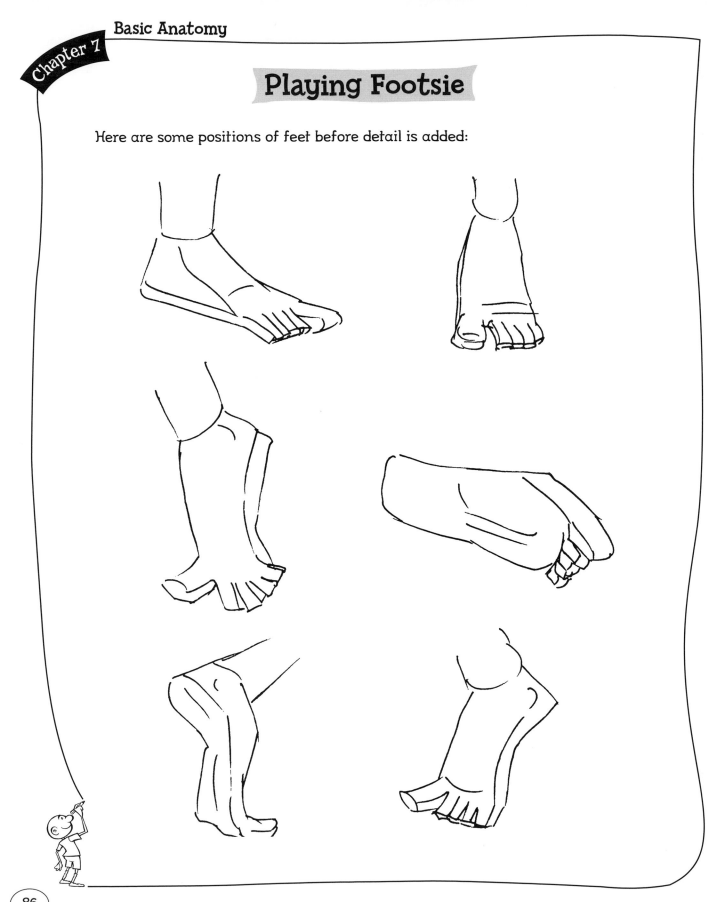

And with some detail added:

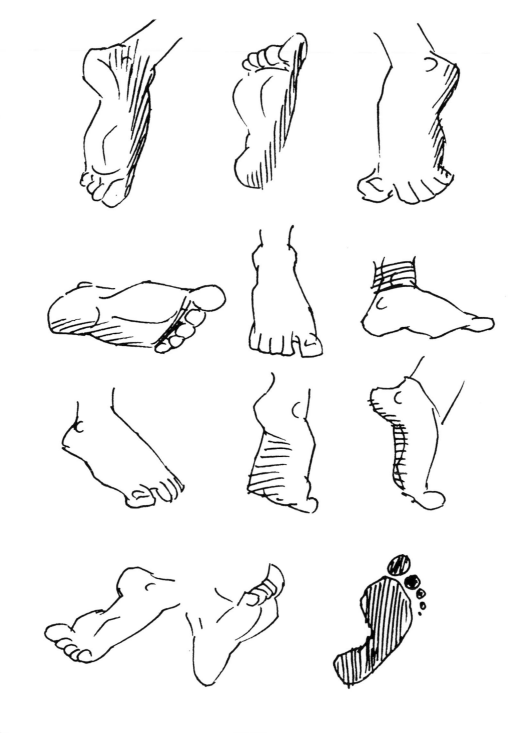

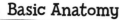

Chapter 7

Body Positions

Define the various body positions of your character before you begin to detail them. This is where the action becomes important.

Doodle Page

Doodle Page

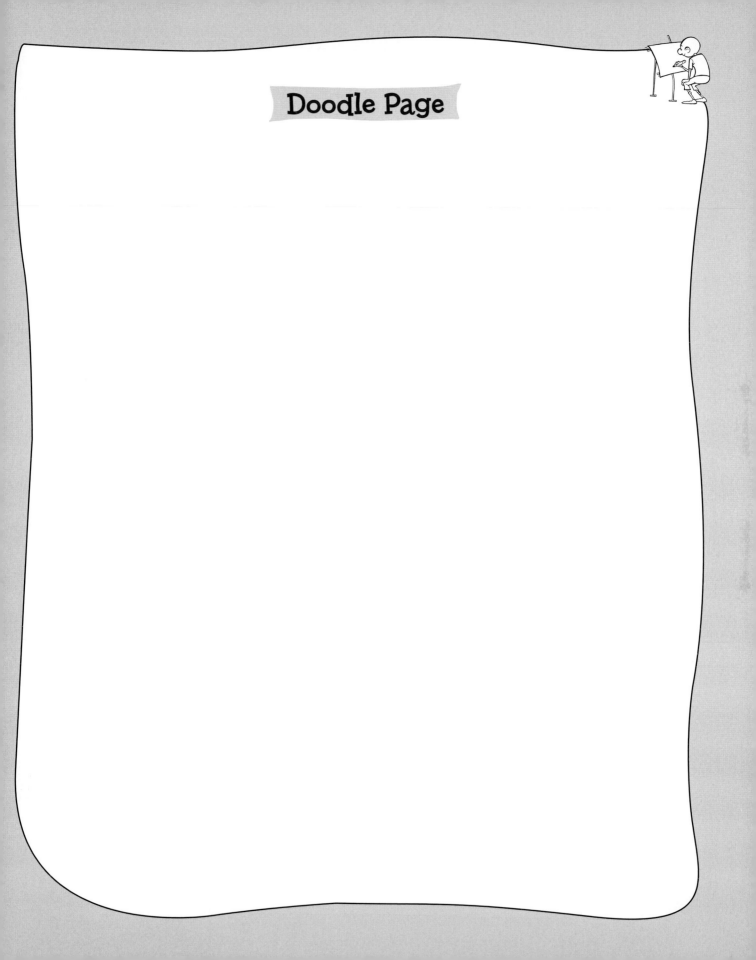

Chapter 8

Drawing with a Reference

Make sure you capture my notes!

Reference Point

When cartooning, it's sometimes a good idea to copy parts of a photograph from a book or a magazine. This is handy when making detailed sketches of automobiles, architectural drawings, streets, etc.

For example, if you're drawing a sports car parked in front of a building, you would need photographs of both the sports car and the building. Always copy from a photograph, never from a drawing or an illustration, or you'll end up losing detail.

Drawing from real life, or reality sketching, is another way to do it. It's a technique used when sketching people or animals, and is especially effective if you're replicating body postures and actions.

Here's a tip: Ask the person modeling for you to act out the postures or actions you want. For example, a model playing golf can hold a club so that you can see exactly how he or she grips the club, positions their feet, and bends forward.

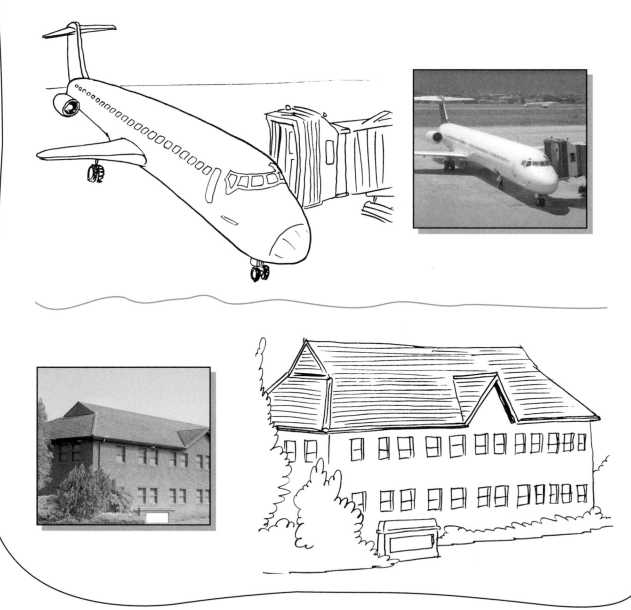

Drawing with a Reference

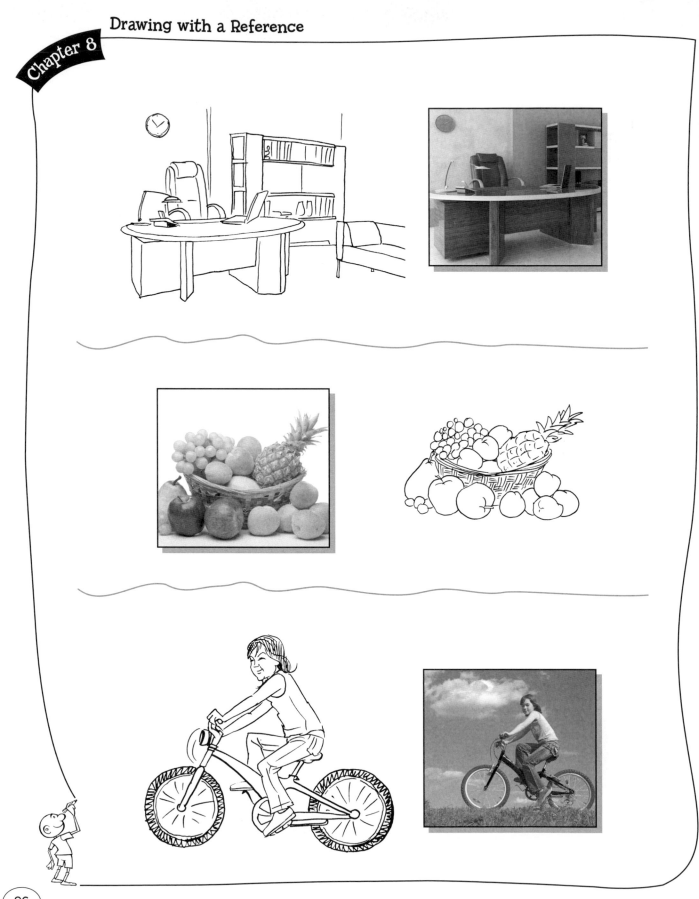

Mixed Media

Sometimes you can use your pictorial references as the base of your cartoon frame. See how the following images can come together with cartoons to create a whole new look.

Chapter 8

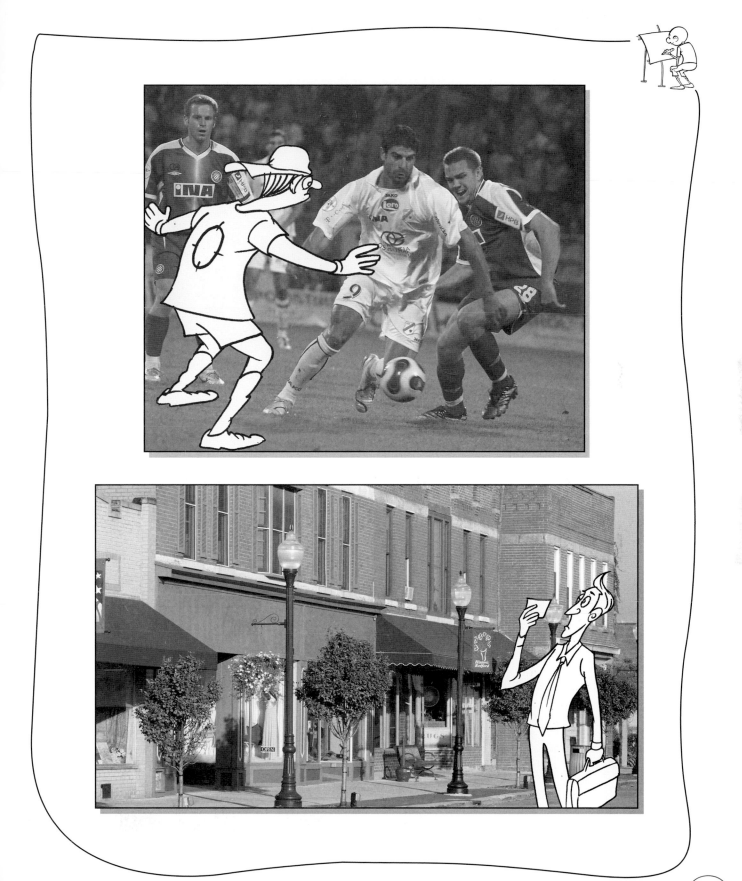

101

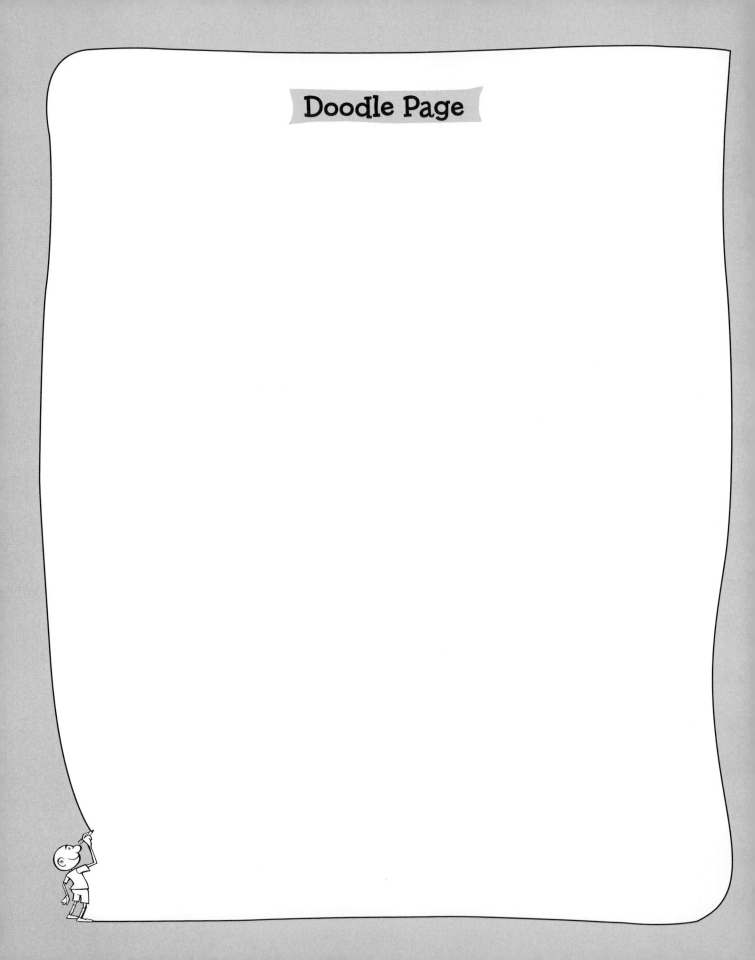

Doodle Page

Doodle Page

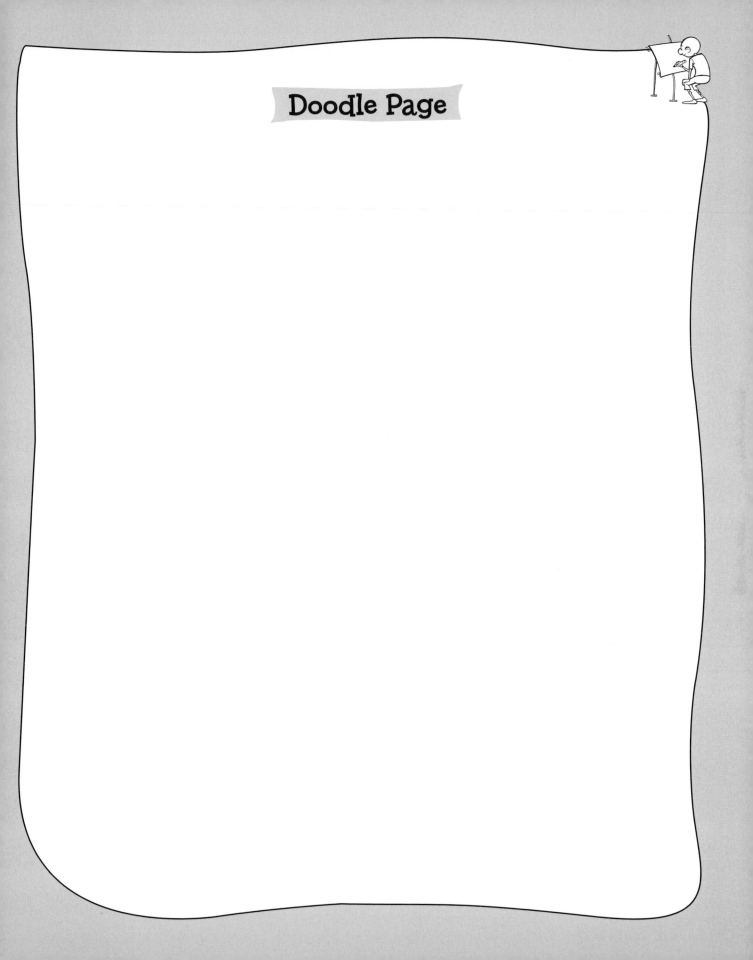

Chapter 9

Tools of the Trade

Hand Tools

No matter how skilled you are, or how imaginative, the drawing tools you choose can make all the difference.

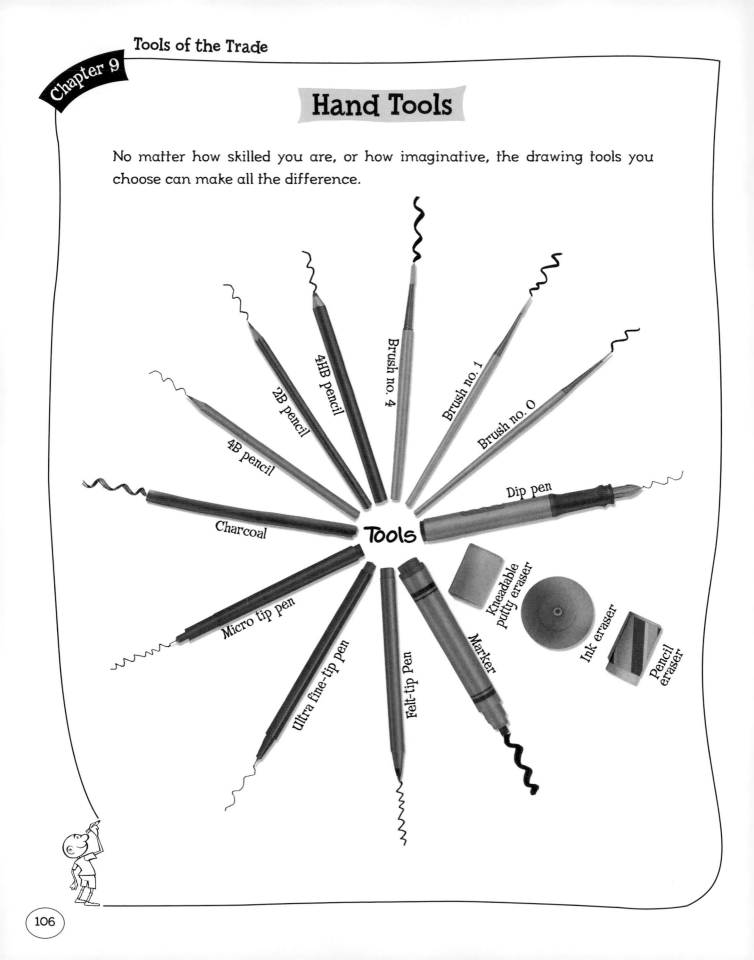

Brush no. 4

4HB pencil

2B pencil

4B pencil

Charcoal

Micro tip pen

Ultra fine-tip pen

Felt-tip Pen

Marker

Tools

Brush no. 1

Brush no. 0

Dip pen

Kneadable putty eraser

Ink eraser

Pencil eraser

Choosing the tool, or mixing it up, could create some fascinating effects. Check out the examples below:

Brush and fine-tip pen

Charcoal

Dip pen

Drawing pencil

Fine-tip pen

Brush

Ink pen

Fine-tip and flat-tip pen

Round marker

Flat-tip marker

Chapter 9

Computer Tools

Go high tech and you'll discover endless possibilities. And no, that's not cheating. There are several software solutions available. Here's how a simple pencil sketch can get dimension with tools and effects.

1 Rough pencil sketch

2 Final pencil sketch

3 Final ink

4 Colored or shaded on the computer

5 With a shadow

6 Light effects

Here are some additional textures that can be created with a computer to make your cartoons more interesting:

Doodle Page

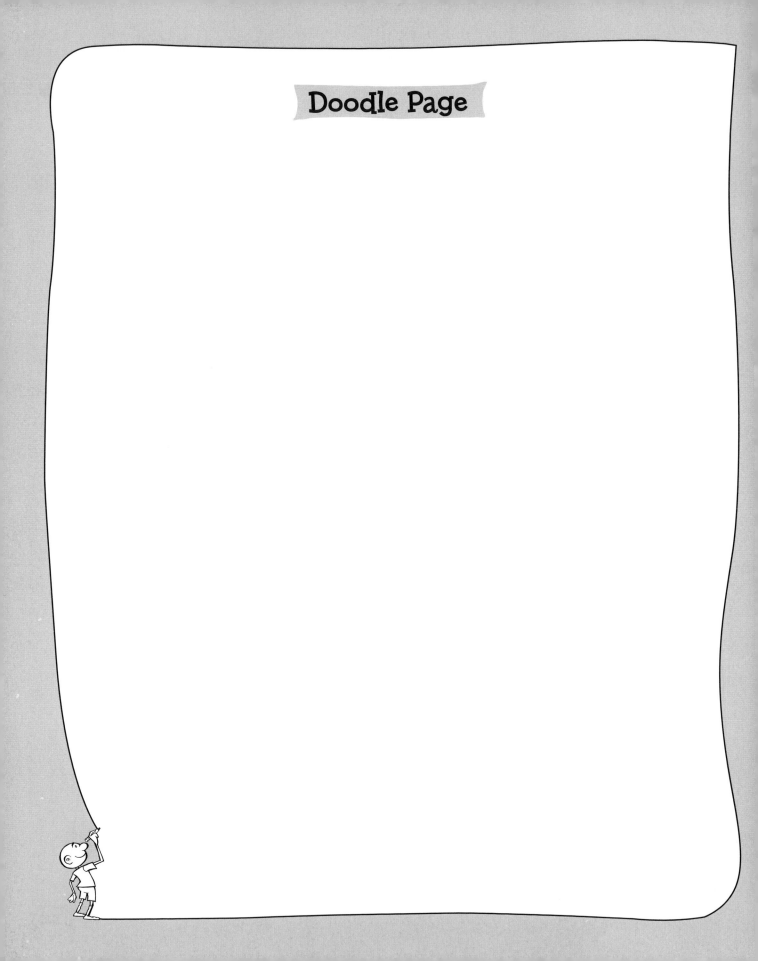

Doodle Page

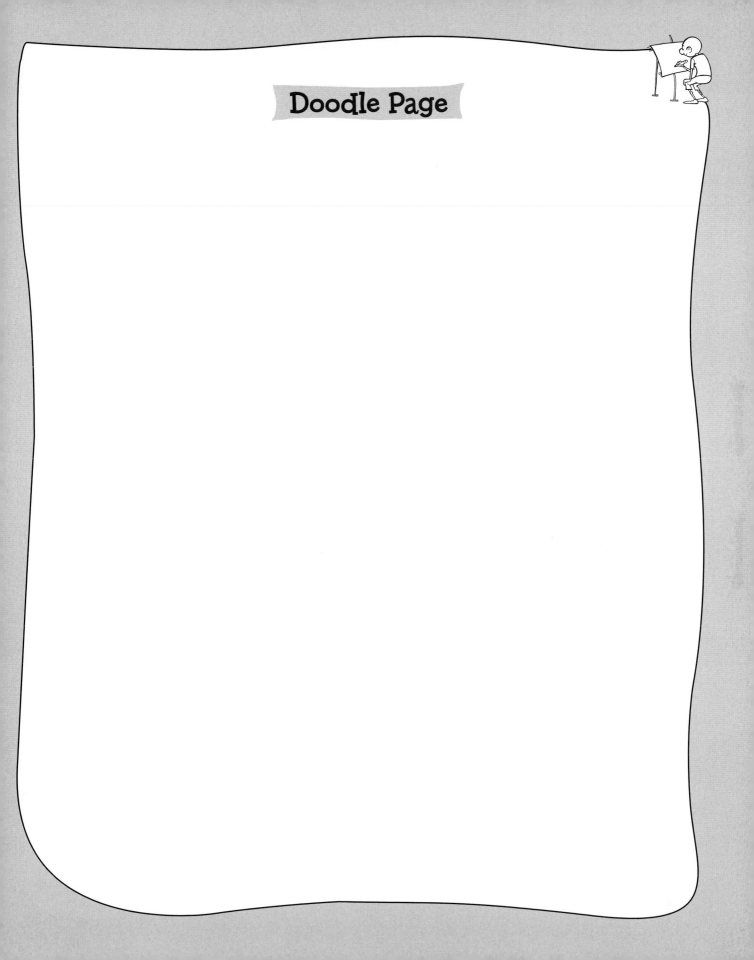

Chapter 10

Developing a Personal Style

Uniquely 'You'

Imagine looking through a prism. Each one of us looks at life through our own prism of perception. No two people see the same thing in the same way.

Similarly, a personal style is the cartoonist's **interpretation of the things he or she sees**—and **the way he or she draws it**. Which is why no two cartoonists will ever think up the same gag or have the same sense of comic timing. Your personal style is your visual signature. And the more distinct your style, the more popular you may become.

Look at the following cartoon style and notice what makes each one unique.

Chapter 10

Guess what? You already HAVE a personal style. All you have to do is keep drawing to discover what it is. Follow the suggestions below and you're almost a pro! In no time, you'll see your own unique style come through.

- Maintain shape, proportions, and structure.

- Construct your characters by using two to three basic shapes only, and use those shapes consistently. For instance, if a particular character's head is oval and his legs are wiry, use those same attributes every time you draw that character.

Developing a Personal Style

Here are some examples of stylized features that make these characters unique:

Blockish body structures and straight lines

Spindly legs and a Pinocchio nose

Exaggerated noses and simplistic figures

Rendering

Use any medium or tool you're comfortable with to render or execute your characters. Then use that tool consistently. This creates a uniform style.

Chapter 10

Shading Your Way

You can also add shading and texture by using **lines, dots,** or **cross-hatching** (intersecting lines). These techniques will give your cartoons an even further distinctiveness.

Here are some more examples of shading techniques:

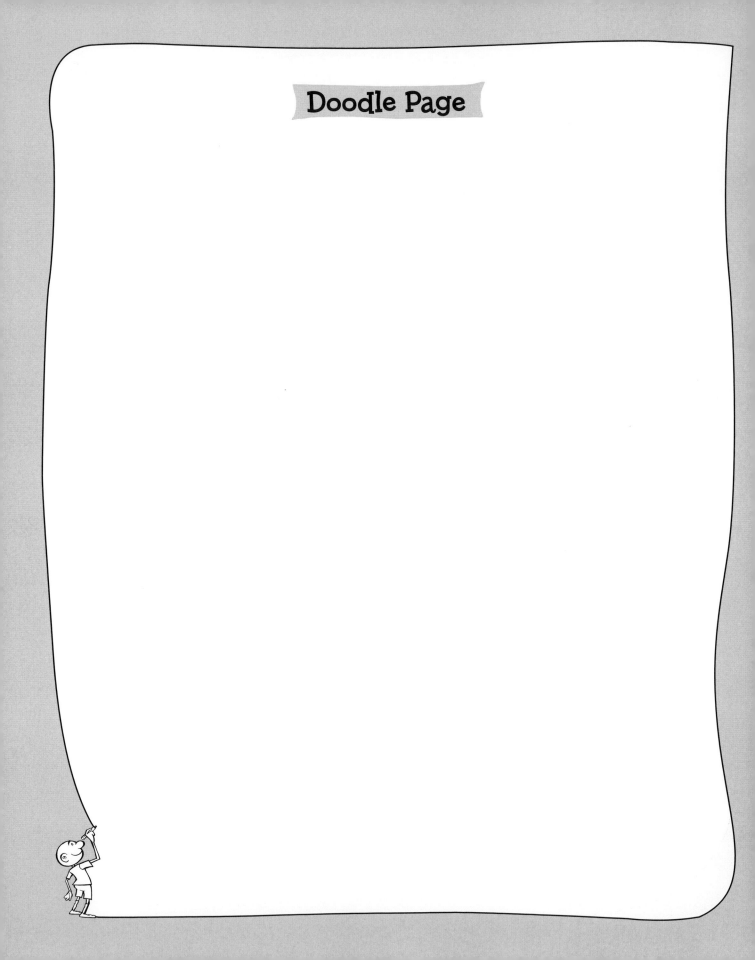

Doodle Page

Doodle Page

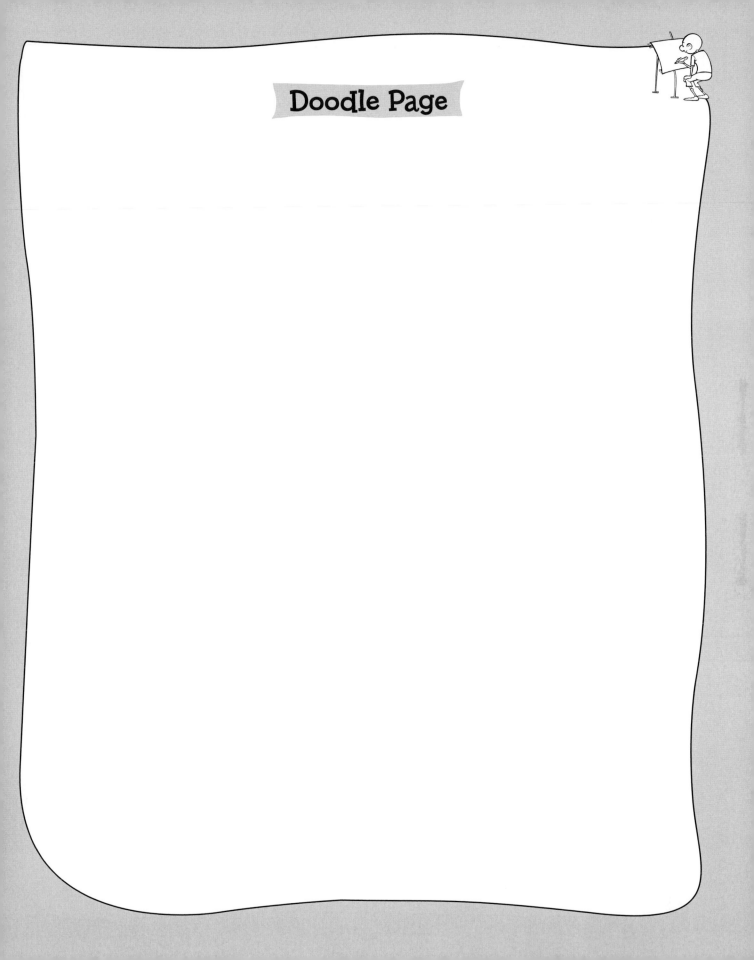

Chapter 11

Composition

Chapter 11

Different Elements

The way you compose your cartoon tells a large part of your story. First, decide on the elements in your composition. Let's take a look at a composition with four elements.

Character

Road

Car

Buildings

Next, ask yourself:

• **What is your setting and your layout?**

• **Is it day or night? Is it a city or a small town?**

• **What is your character doing in the scene?**

Reference Point

Notice how the reference point of the composition makes it more interesting.

Daytime: character approaches office building

Composition

Situation

Evening: character drives home

Mood

What is the mood of your illustration?

Is the character looking forward to going home?

Or has he been fired and is feeling dejected?

Aesthetics

It's easier to get your point across when the elements are arranged in a pleasing manner.

Always avoid:

Too much white space

Scattered elements

Too rational

An ideal balance:

Balance

Balance is easily achieved by arranging the elements of your composition carefully, and by varying their sizes and positions. Make sure you balance the light and the dark areas of your composition. For instance, avoid too much shading on one side unless it is balanced by a black area on the other side.

Too little shading

Too much shading

Balanced shading

Perspective

Here are some basic rules to help you get your perspective right.

1. As an object moves further away from the eye, it appears smaller.

2. As an object moves closer to the eye, it appears larger.

3. Horizontal lines above eye level appear to move downward as they move farther away from the eye.

4. Horizontal lines below eye level appear to move upward as they move farther away from the eye.

Eye level

Imagined horizon

5. Horizontal lines running in the same direction meet at a point in the distance called the **"vanishing point."**

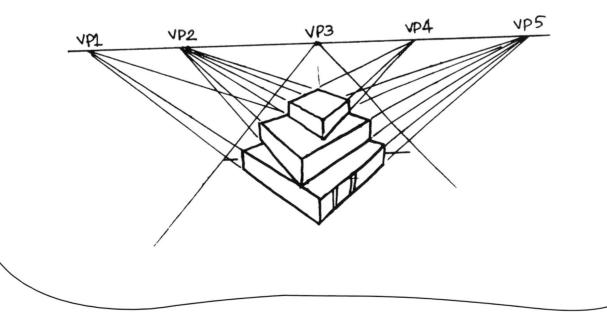

Doodle Page

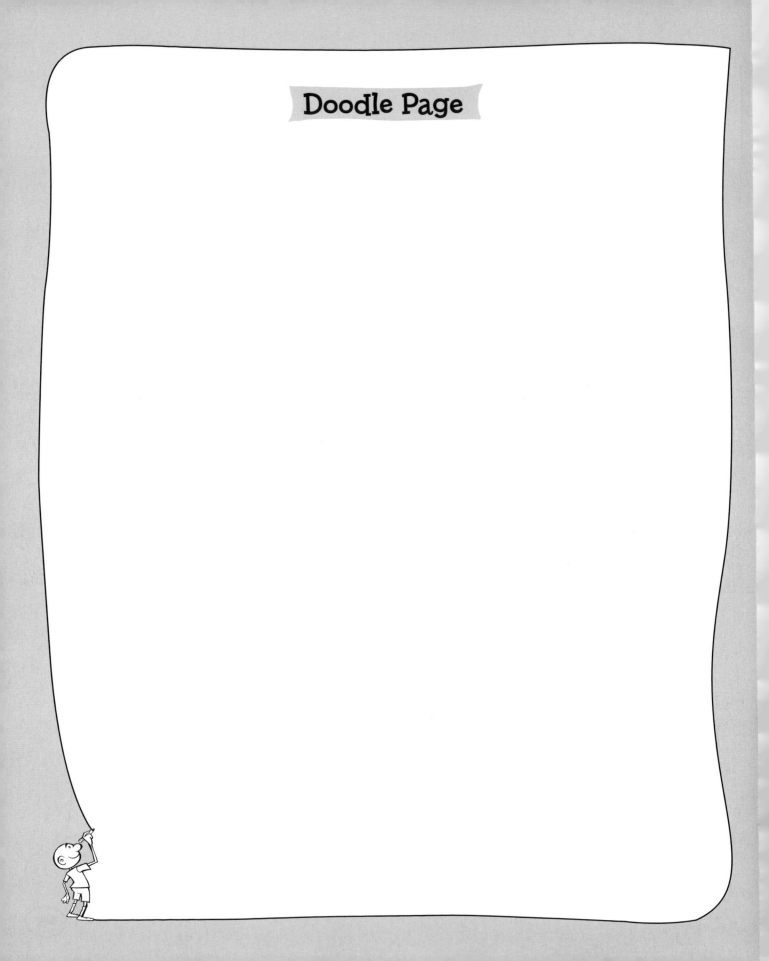

3. Horizontal lines above eye level appear to move downward as they move farther away from the eye.

4. Horizontal lines below eye level appear to move upward as they move farther away from the eye.

Eye level
Imagined horizon

5. Horizontal lines running in the same direction meet at a point in the distance called the **"vanishing point."**

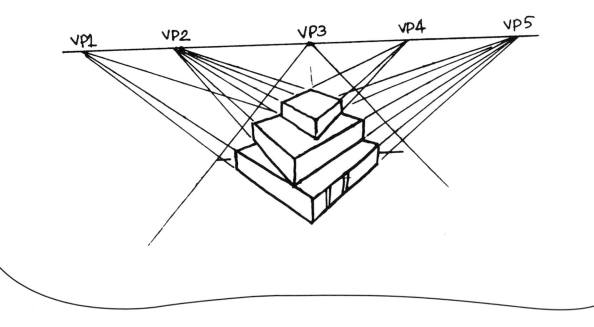

You can apply the rules of perspective AFTER deciding where to place the elements in your illustration. Some cartoonists draw in perspective by instinct.

While your drawing must have a sense of perspective, but you do not need to draw absolutely straight parallel lines. For example, in the image below, a man is looking at some pictures on the wall. Since the style is loose and free flowing, the lines are not straight but the pictures are getting smaller in distance.

Close-up perspective

Distance perspective

Rear perspective—from behind

Floor-up perspective—from below

Some guidelines to help you achieve your perspective.

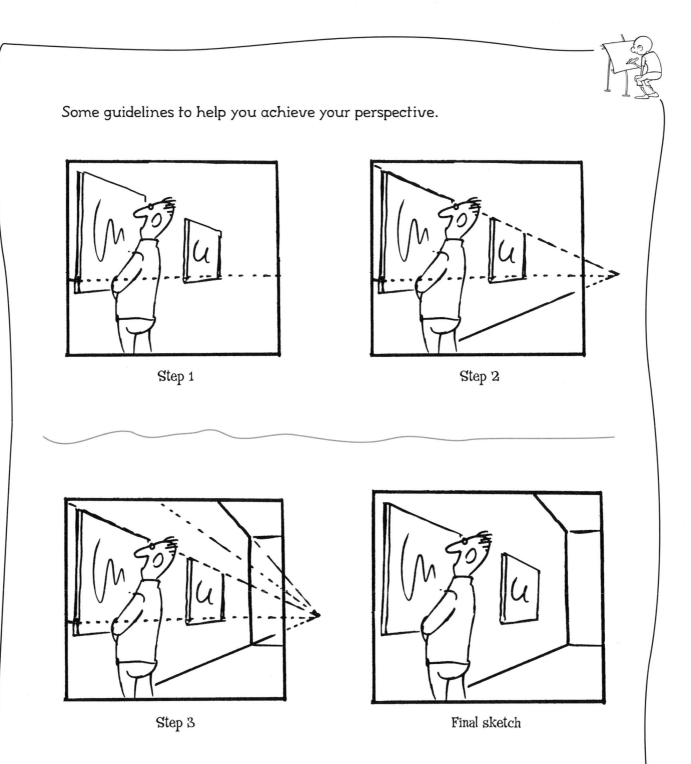

Step 1

Step 2

Step 3

Final sketch

Here's a tip: When you start drawing, sketch the lines meeting at a vanishing point BEFORE you start constructing the perpendicular lines. That way, you will get the perspective right.

Doodle Page

Doodle Page

Chapter 12

Types of Cartoons

Types of Cartoons

Types of cartoons go by different names depending on their style and purpose, but they're all meant to tease the imagination. You're probably most familiar with **the gag** or **box cartoon**. It's what you see in the newspaper every day.

Gag Cartoons

Box Cartoons

Comic Strips

A comic strip is a sequence of drawings that tells a story. Comic strips are often featured daily and weekly in newpapers and magazines.

Chapter 12

Comic Books

A comic book is a magazine or book that contains narrative artwork, dialog, and descriptive prose. While subject matter in comic books is often humorous, it can also be serious, suspenseful, and action-packed.

Graphic Novels

A graphic novel is a type of comic book, usually with a storyline similar to a novel. The term **graphic novel** is not strictly defined, and is constantly evolving. However, it often suggests a story that has a beginning, middle, and end, as opposed to a comic strip or book that has an ongoing series with continuing characters. Graphic novels are characteristically created in longer formats than comic magazines, and are often aimed at mature audiences.

Doodle Page

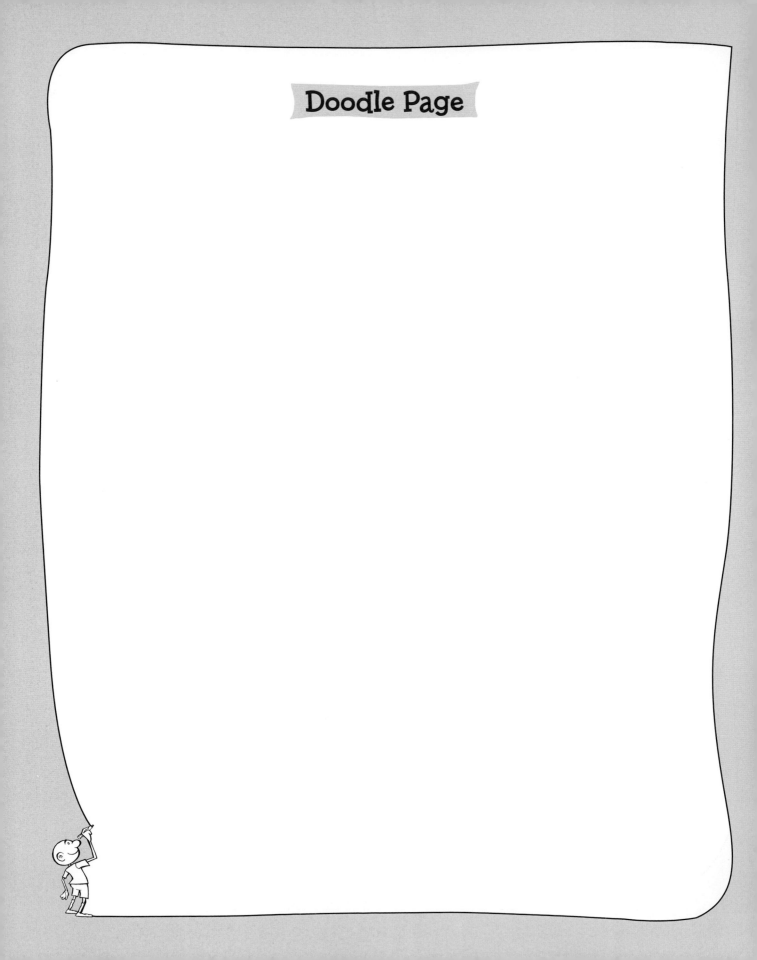

Doodle Page

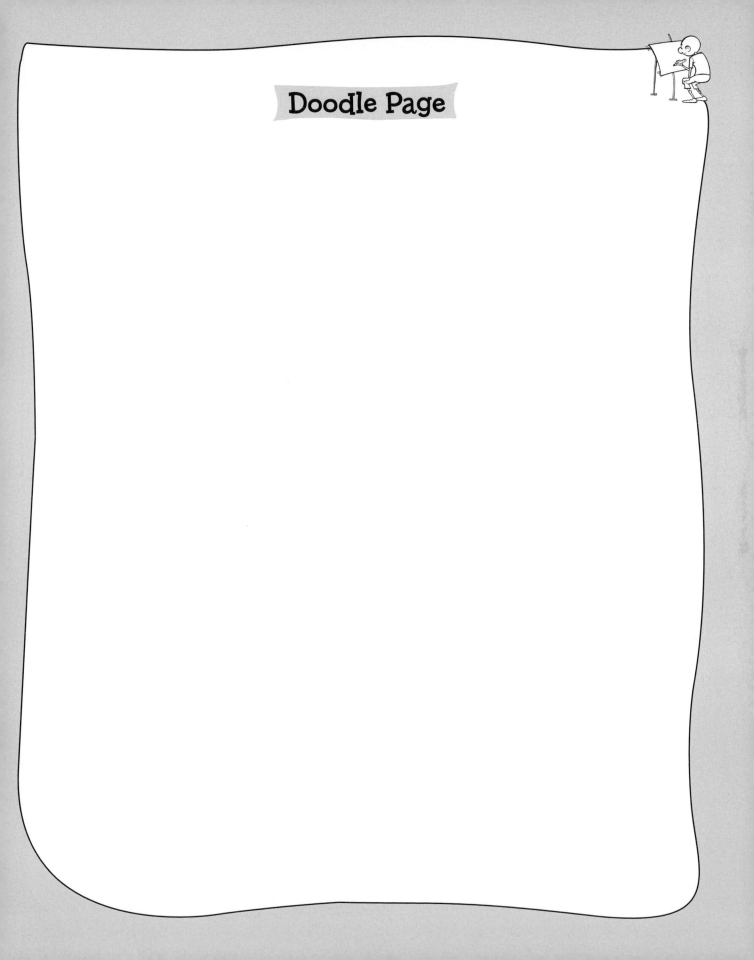

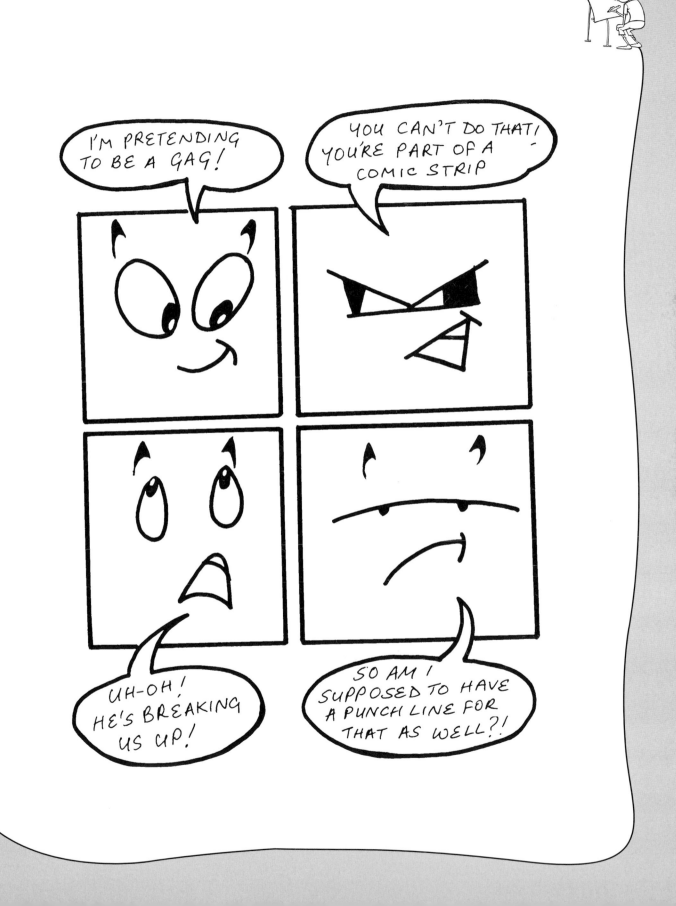

Visual Punch Lines

Gag cartoons are easy to draw. All you have to do is think up a punch line and an accompanying visual to tell the rest of the story. The punch line and visual work together to complement each other. The characters' expressions and actions are critical to making it work. Remember, **just as the punch line must be succinct, the illustration must be simple, not elaborate**.

Here are some gag cartoons:

Generating Ideas

Ideas spring out of everywhere and seemingly nowhere—while you're singing in the shower, driving, or shopping. Begin by thinking up a punch line. That takes writing skills, but don't panic! It's easier to write jokes than you realize. Think the unexpected, and imagine a gag situation. The encyclopedia and Internet are both good resources for ideas.

Here are some sample gag situations:

Visual   Gag

Visual   Gag

Making Your Words and Pictures Speak

Writing gags

Don't just sit there, start writing! Now that you have a situation, think of a funny line to accompany it.

Visual

Gag

Visual

Gag

Tips

There are no real rules to thinking up a gag, but here are some suggestions that might help. Ask yourself:

• How can the situation be exaggerated?

• What are the characters saying to the viewer and to each other?

• Can the scene be set in another place or in the future or past?

• Is there a reference to any event in the news or in history?

• Can it be relevant to current issues such as the environment or politics?

Let your mind roam free; shake up your imagination. Here are some words that make for a starting point for a gag:

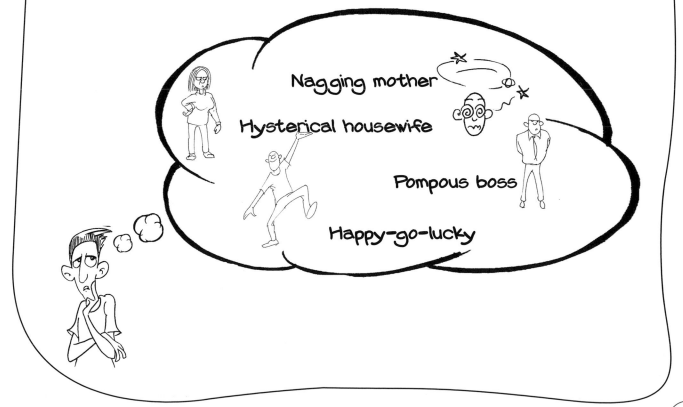

Nagging mother

Hysterical housewife

Pompous boss

Happy-go-lucky

If free associating doesn't work, try doodling aimlessly, and then think up a funny line for your doodles. Take a look at the doodles below, and explore the potential for a gag.

Fish flying in the sky

A deserted island

A rocket taking off

A man with a big heart

Doodle Boards

Doodle boards are sketches for your cartoon ideas. You can make several doodles of the same gag situations on your doodle board. This will help you pick the best way to visually represent your gag. Some examples:

Idea Bank

Here are some sample situations you can use for gags:

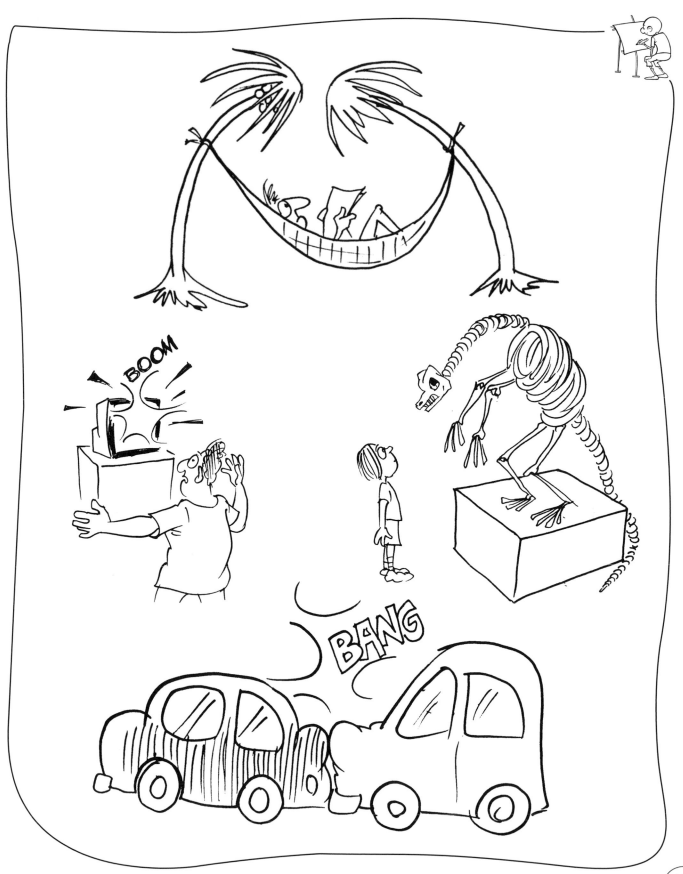

Doodle Page

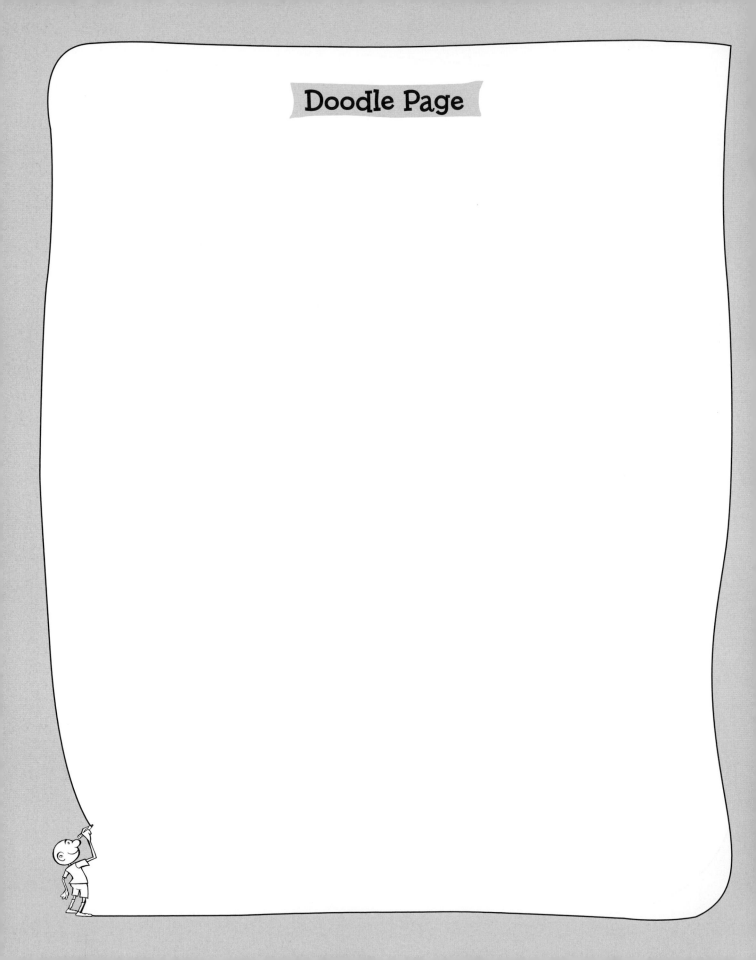

Doodle Page

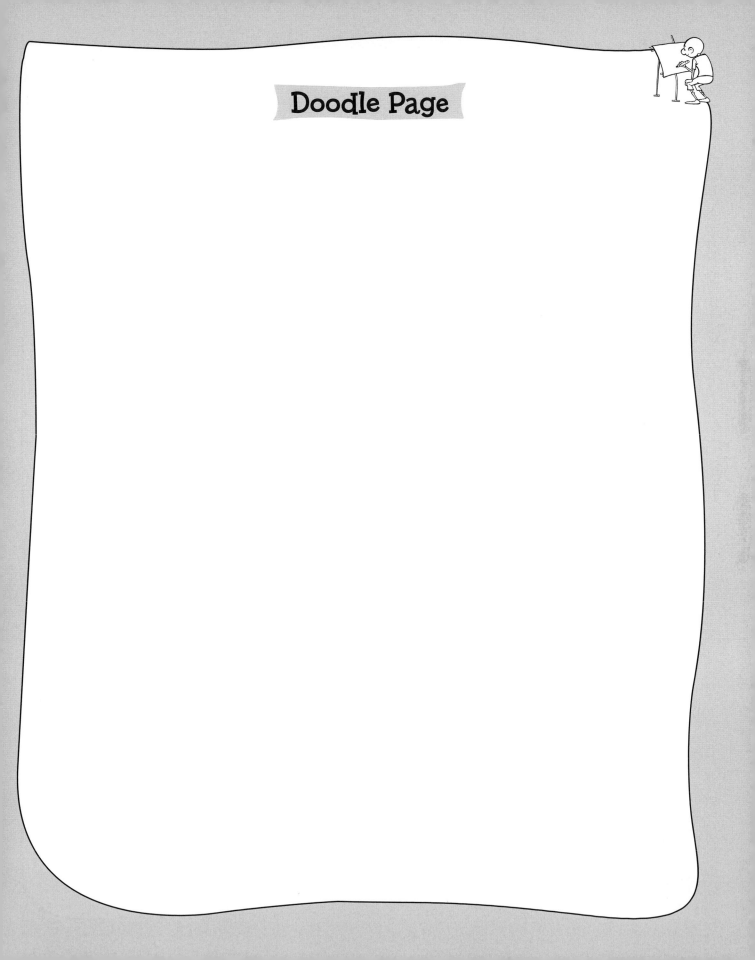

Chapter 14

Caricatures

Physical Features

A caricature is an illustration that distorts or exaggerates certain features of a person to create an easily identifiable likeness.

Drawing caricatures is fun. Start by picking **one unique, distinguishing feature** of a person, and exaggerate it. Begin with a basic shape, and then add humor to it.

Here's how it's done:

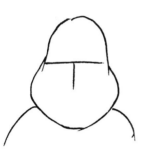

①

②

③

④

⑤

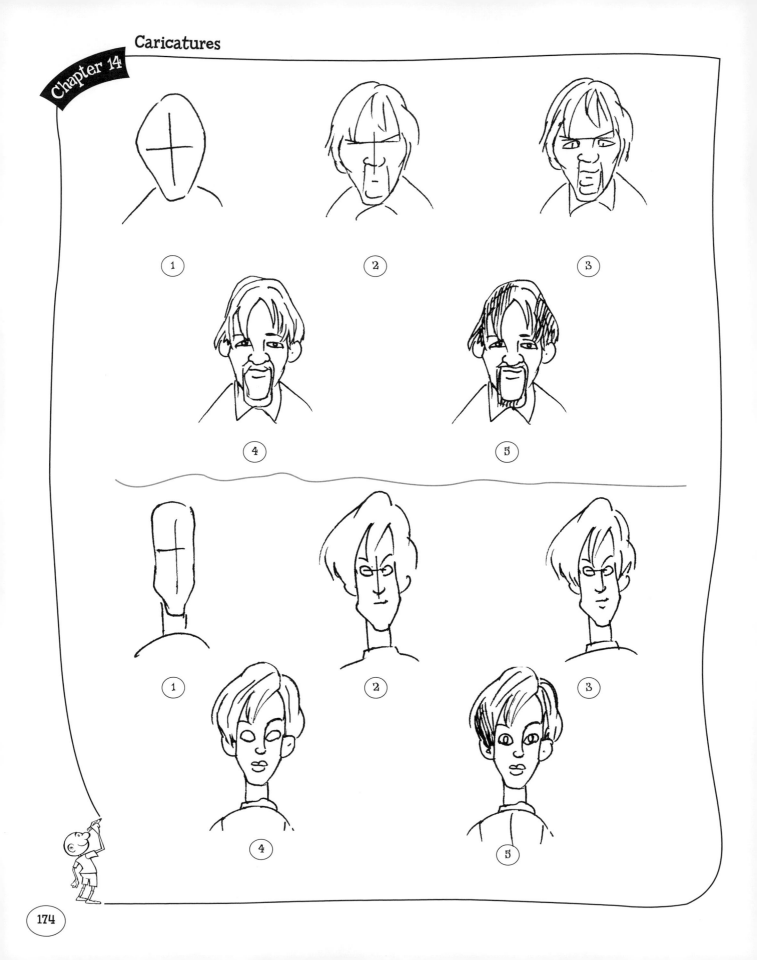

Caricatures

Tips

It is often helpful to take a real portrait and place it to the side of your doodle board. Then take a long, hard look at the features on the character's face. Next, imagine looking at the portrait through a convex or concave lens!

Here are a few examples:.

Mahatma Gandhi

Prince Charles

Jim Carrey

Elvis Presley

Mr. Bean

Madonna

Charlie Chaplin

David Beckham

Political Cartoons

Take a look at the morning newspaper and you can usually find a political cartoon. Political cartoons often poke fun at politicians and find humor in news and current affairs. They are a good way to help readers remember important news events.

Doodle Page

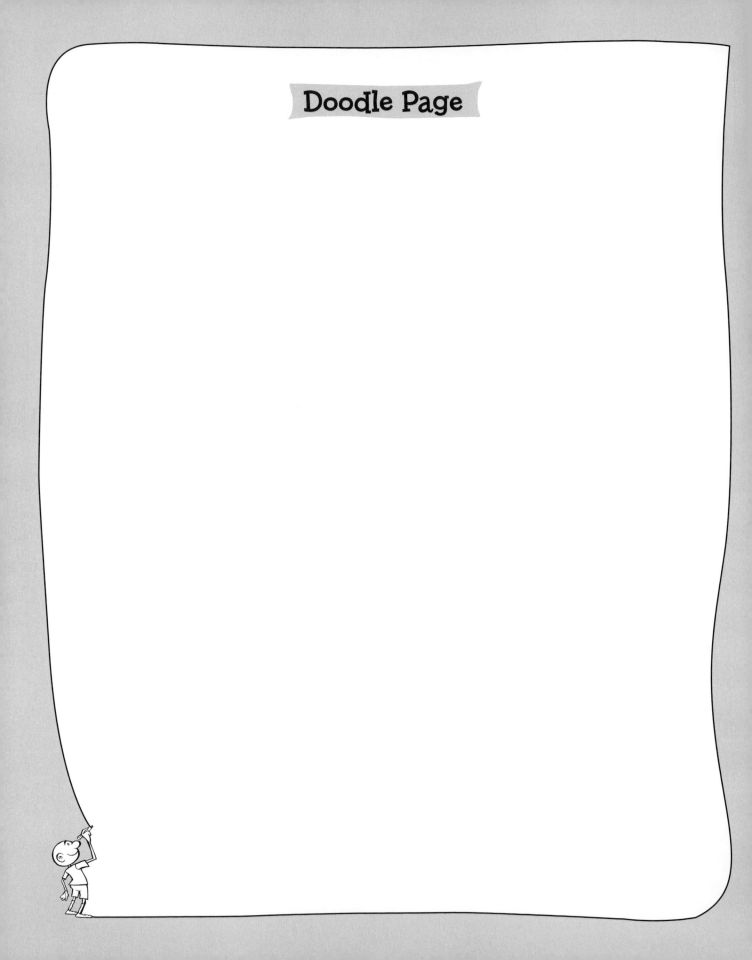

Doodle Page

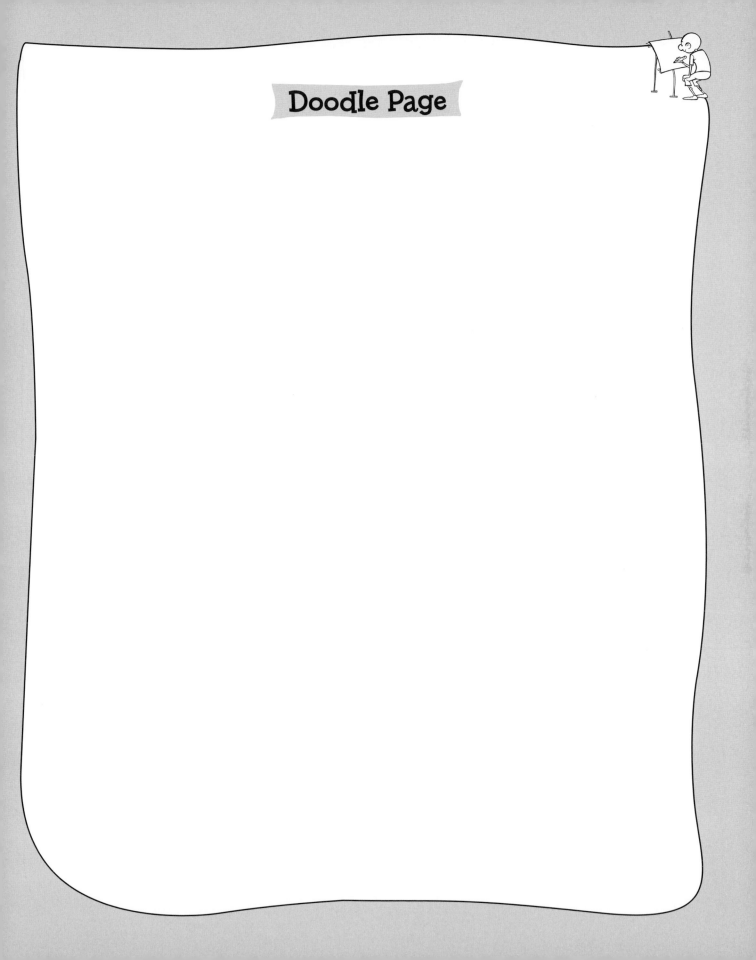

Chapter 15

Comic Strips

Comic Strips

Comic strips are usually made up of **three or four box drawings** in sequence, each depicting a part of the story as it unfolds. The fourth or last box has **a punch line**, which concludes the story.

The closest the comic strip comes to any other art form is the storyboards created for movies and commercials.

The Gag Strip

A gag strip usually appears as a single row of drawings in the daily newspaper. It is usually in **black and white**. On special days, several gag strips appear in two to three rows, often in color.

The following are some examples:

Generating Ideas

You can start your comic strip by making a doodle board. Keep drawing your characters from different angles at different locations and see where it leads. Don't worry about the size and placement of the illustrations just yet. Just experiment with what YOU think is funny. Eventually, you'll hit upon a drawing or story line around which you can weave the entire strip.

Don't fret; the ideas will eventually flow. Once you get the hang of it, you can draw many more characters in different situations and make many more comic strips!

Lying upside down on a sofa

Watching TV

Gossiping with the neighbor through the window

Having a very tall sandwich on his plate

Mopping the floor

Cooking

Mowing the lawn

Nagging

Now that you've got your characters and the setting (in this case, a couple at home), simply make it all add up. Using the same story line, mix it up in your imagination and vary the ideas!

Here are a few more comic strips based on the above situation:

Writing the Strip

Once you have the punch line, you can build up the story that leads up to it. Let's see what we can do with one of the punch lines on the previous page.

Comic Timing and Sequencing

Comic timing means knowing exactly how to place the visuals and text so that the punch line has, well, punch!

There are several ways to do this:

- One way is to write the strip so that there is **a text pause in the third box**. This means there's either minimal or no text in the box.

- Another way is to include **a visual punch line in the fourth box**.

Text in caption boxes
to describe the setting

Text in blurbs
or speech
bubbles

Text as visual or
special effects

There are two ways to add lettering—**hand lettering** and **typesetting**. Hand lettering is recommended unless you want to typeset the text on the computer and then cut and paste it on your artwork. Not only is this time-consuming, it is also not as accurate as hand lettering.

Once you have drawn the visuals in each box in pencil, draw the blurbs next to the characters and estimate how much space the text will occupy. The blurbs may have to spill onto the visual if the text takes up too much space.

Handwrite the text inside the blurbs, spacing out the letters so that the words are legible. Capital letters are the easiest to read.

If you must write in upper and lowercase, do not use your own handwriting—it takes longer to read.

Use neat, evenly spaced letters. You can draw horizontal guidelines with a ruler to make sure the height of the letters is uniform. You can also measure the space between the lines to ensure even spacing.

Lettering Special Effects

You can use a variety of **visual effects** in lettering. Keep a reference of the type you want to use. Decide how you want to layout the letters in the word—horizontally, vertically, along a curve, or in perspective. Accordingly, draw guidelines in pencil. Draw the letters, using your typeface as a reference for each letter.

You can either outline the letters or use solid letters. For a thin outline, you could use **a thin-nib pen**, or you can use **a bold marker** directly over your penciled letters.

Lettering Tools and Techniques

Your choice of tools for lettering is crucial. You cannot expect to write legibly with a sable brush!

That leaves us with **technical pens** (pens used for architectural drawings), **dip pens** (where the pen has a nib that is dipped in ink before writing), and **markers** (for bold lettering). Make sure the ink you use can be covered up by correction fluid in case you make mistakes.

Comic Strip Language

Telling it like it is doesn't mean saying it any which way you can. It's an art. Comic strip language is very similar to cartoon language as discussed earlier. Expressions like **"Gasp!"**, **"Aargh!"**, and **"Sigh!"** are common to both. But with comic strips, you can place lettering effects between two boxes. Also, a comic strip can tell an entire story through pictures only—text is not a must!

Doodle Page

Doodle Page

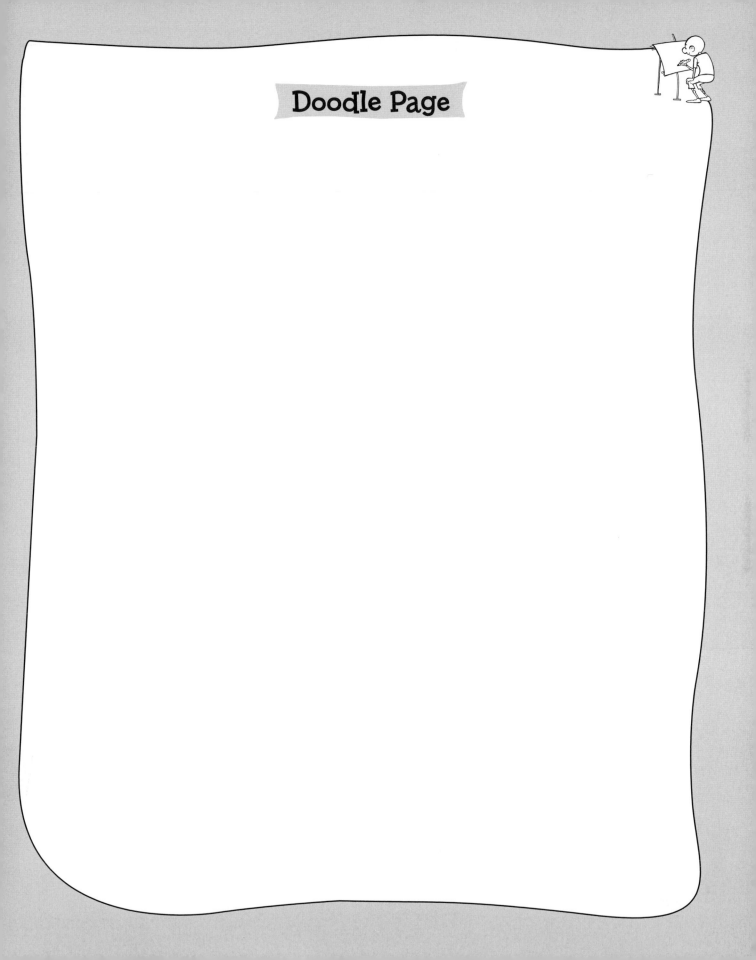

Chapter 16

Comic Books

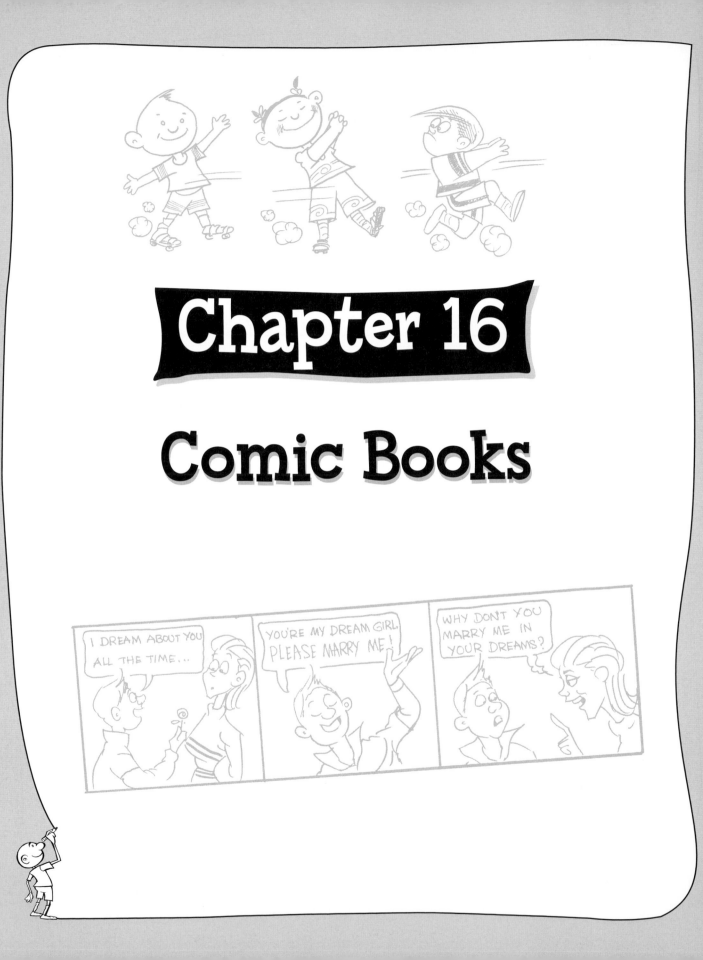

Types of Comic Books

The standard comic book comprises thirty-two pages, front and back covers, all printed in color. There are variations like paperbacks, covers in color with the rest in black and white, etc.

There are different types of comic books depending on the kind of reader. Comic books for children are different from **superhero books** meant for older children or teens. There are also **horror comic books, science fiction comic books**, and **comic books that are movie adaptations**. Each type follows its own style and genre.

Story Lines

The stories in comics differ according to the profile of the reader and type of comic book. Superhero comic books tackle subjects like good vs. evil, superheroes saving the planet, and adventure stories.

Comic books for young children are often about children's daily activities and usually are set in places such as school or the park. They can be educational, too.

Drawing

Drawing for a comic book is much more complex than drawing a comic strip. But don't let that scare you! Once you write the story, prepare a page plan. That is, decide how much and which portion of the story will appear on each page as well as the number of boxes on each page. Next, plan the content of each box, including visual and textual elements. After that, detail each individual box—draw the visual and plan the spaces for the text.

Penciling

For comic books, there are dedicated artists to execute each task of the production process. There are a set of artists who do the penciling for each book, another set for the inking, and yet another set for the coloring. The penciling is done first. Artists who do the penciling create the visual structure of the book. Drawings are usually executed proportionately larger than the final dimensions before they are reduced during the printing process. As a rule, they are drawn fifty percent larger.

Finished Outline

The penciled work is usually a finished drawing with clear lines so that the inking artist can clearly see where to put his or her lines. Shading with a pencil turned on its side is an absolute no-no!

Basic inking

Rendering/styling

Coloring

Tools

To draw, ink, and color comic books, you will need **a light box to trace** and **an inclined board**. This will spare your back, if you plan to be a successful artist!

There is an array of pens you can use, but make sure to use black India ink, as all inking is done in India ink. India ink produces a high density of black without leaving transparent patches.

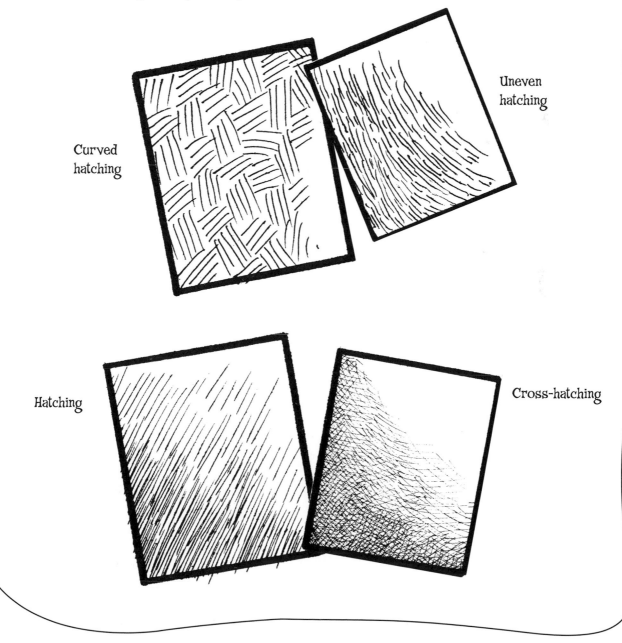

Curved hatching

Uneven hatching

Hatching

Cross-hatching

Brushes are also used extensively for inking. The number of the brush or its thickness determines on the thickness of the line. Use **smooth drawing paper,** **watercolor paper,** or **illustration boards**. You will also need an **X-ACTO knife** to cut out the textured sticker papers in the neat and precise shapes required.

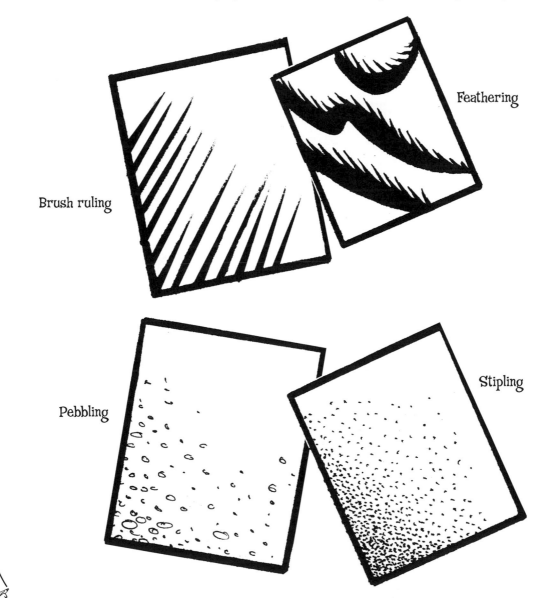

Feathering

Brush ruling

Stipling

Pebbling

Finally, you will need a computer to type out the story (if you're writing it yourself) and to color the images.

Brush & pen

Sketch pen

Dip pen & ink

227

Doodle Page

Doodle Page

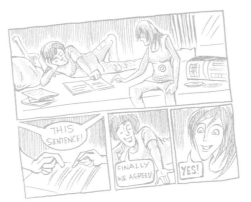

Chapter 17

Graphic Novels

Target Audience

If you're planning to write and illustrate your own graphic novel, it's important to start by identifying your readers. Ask yourself these questions:

- What is the target age group?
- What are they reading?
- What catches their interest on TV and the Internet?
- What kind of music do they listen to?
- What is their primary occupation?

Once you answer these questions, you can decide your **story line** and what **kind of illustration style** to use.

Writing the Story

Rule number one: **Write for yourself** rather than the reader. Write about things close to your heart and concerns that may be shared by potential readers.

Do keep in mind that the genre of the graphic novel boasts many books of literary value.

There are two basic ways in which scripts are handled:

• The writer and the artist may be the same person.

• The script may be completed entirely by the writer and then handed over to the artist to illustrate.

To help you along, here's some jargon common to both films and graphic novels. These terms are used to describe the type of illustration in the box or frame.

Establishing Shot: An illustration of a place or location which tells the reader where the story is set.

Long Shot: A distant view of the place or location.

Close-up Shot: An image of a subject at close range.

Head and shoulders shot: An image of a subject with only head and shoulders visible.

Establishing Shot

Long Shot

Close-up Shot 1

Close-up Shot 2

Head and Shoulders Shot

Format

You can use many formats for your graphic novel. It may be fully illustrated with frames from the top to the bottom of each page, or it may be partly illustrated, where some of the pages have text like a regular book and the illustrations appear at intervals on half or full pages.

Chapter 17

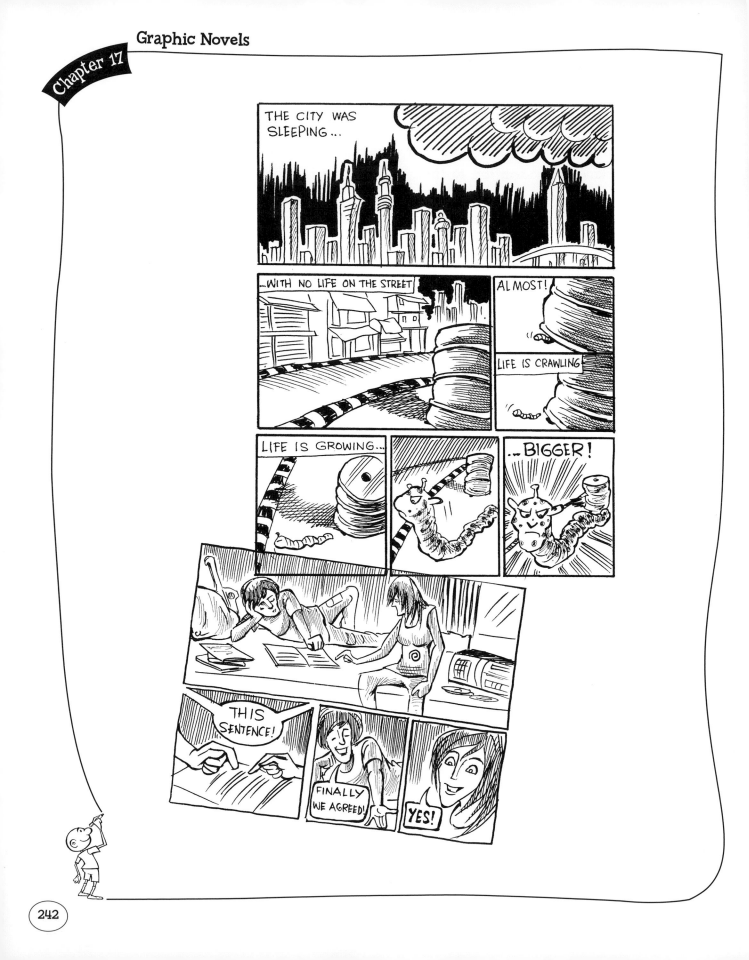

Sequencing

When writing your story, it's important to keep in mind that the sequencing must follow a logical order.

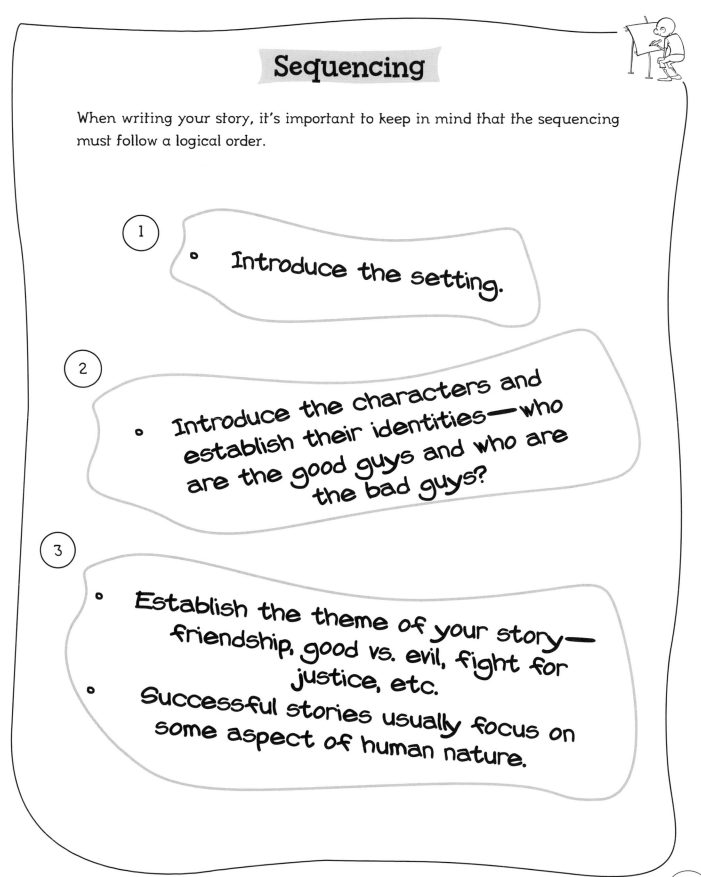

1
- Introduce the setting.

2
- Introduce the characters and establish their identities—who are the good guys and who are the bad guys?

3
- Establish the theme of your story—friendship, good vs. evil, fight for justice, etc.
- Successful stories usually focus on some aspect of human nature.

While breaking down the story, remember that each box shows the characters in action as well as what they're saying. To avoid overcrowding, **do not have more than two speech bubbles in each box**. This means the writing must be concise. Use **fewer words to communicate**. There could also be some **boxes with no dialogue at all**.

Final Layout

Page Layout

You can layout the page of a graphic novel in several ways, depending on the type of book it is.

Manga comics have a distinct style, while superhero comics follow another. The graphic novel could follow any of these or one designed specially for that particular novel, depending on the flow of the story.

Here are some standard rules to split a page into boxes:

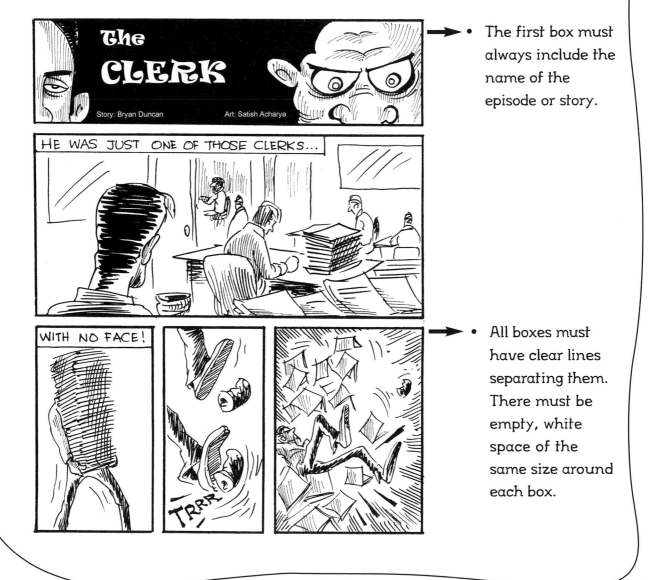

• The first box must always include the name of the episode or story.

• All boxes must have clear lines separating them. There must be empty, white space of the same size around each box.

Chapter 17

Coloring

Coloring with effects

Making It Move

The animation industry uses several techniques to create movement.

In hand-drawn animation, the character or object in motion is drawn at a standard rate of **twenty-four frames per second**. This means that for each second of movement on film, there are **twenty-four illustrations of the character**.

This method allows for **wildly exaggerated movements** and you can squash or stretch the character more than in any other method.

Once you've filled in each page of the book, flip the pages with your thumb and watch your character in action!

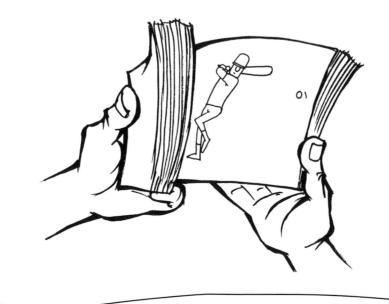

Backgrounds

Backgrounds are critical because they are the setting of your animated film. A background is the place where your character acts out your story. Backgrounds can be illustrated in different ways depending on the style of the film. Some of the most beautiful backgrounds have been done for the classic animation films we grew up with. You need to research backgrounds and it is useful to maintain a reference library of pictures. You can categorize them thus: landscapes, castles, city roads, tall buildings, city streets, beaches, mountains, etc.

269

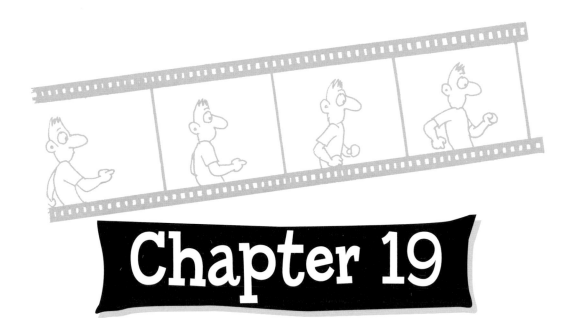

Chapter 19

The Cartoon Market

The Cartoon Market

There's a global market in cartoons out there that is alive and kicking. You need to figure out what kind of work you enjoy and how to classify it. After that, you can begin to present your work to companies operating within that specific category.

Newspapers

Newspapers use **daily and weekend strips**. To practice, you can try imitating one of your favorite comic strips or try a new style.

Magazines

Magazines use cartoon illustrations for **their articles, as well as gags** if they have a humor page.

Most magazines use only one strip. Weekend newspaper magazines may use **gag and political cartoons, comic strips,** and **cartoon illustrations**.

Comic Books and Graphic Novels

Most of these require **realistic styles**. If that is what you are good at, you could fit into their drawing/penciling, inking, or coloring departments.

If you like the more **juvenile style**, there are also some teen and kids' comics where you could find a match.

Comic book covers

Comic book interiors

The Internet

You can also approach **Web sites** to use your strips, gags, or animation clips, as long as the subject matter or theme is consistent with that of the Web site.

Many publications in print have Web sites under the same banner. So a newspaper that uses political cartoons would use them on their Web site as well.

Cartoon Syndicates (Distributers)

It's a good idea to approach a cartoon syndicate or an agent, as they have access to numerous editors and can distribute your comic strip to several newspapers simultaneously. The bigger the syndicating company, the wider their distribution network.

Animation

Animation has many applications depending on the type of animation you like to do. Some of them are:

- animated films
- advertising films
- Web animation
- multimedia animation—CD-ROMs, cell phones, Internet etc.
- animation for TV shows

Animation for TV shows

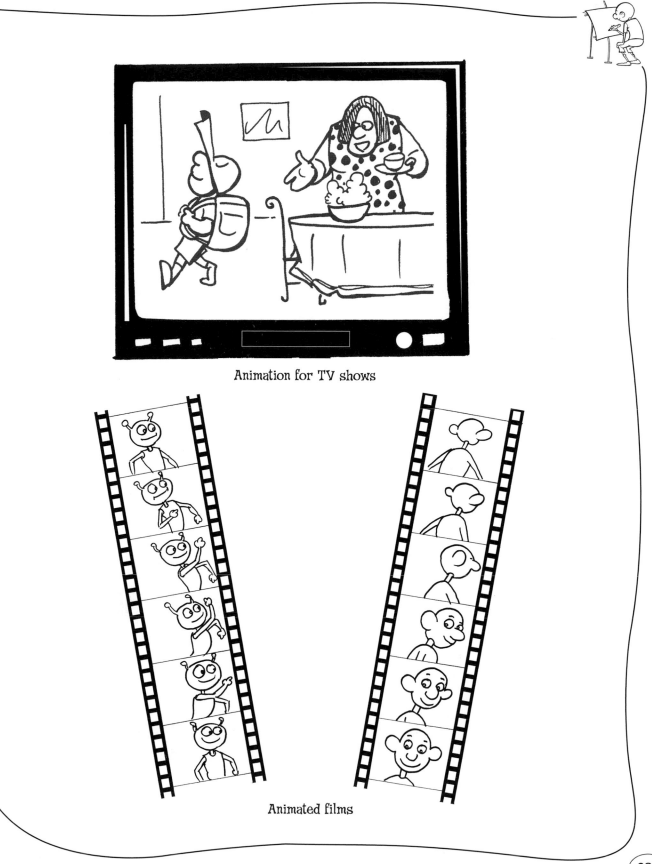

Animation for TV shows

Animated films

The Cartoon Market

Other media:

Magazine

Business card

Photo frame

T-shirt

SMILE

MOTEL MOLY

Signboard

Mug

Greeting Card Companies

If you create gags, greeting card companies can use your work. They can also use it for **e-greetings**.

Since there are several occasions for greeting cards, you could be making gags for all kinds of situations!

T-shirt

Signboard

Mug

Greeting Card Companies

If you create gags, greeting card companies can use your work. They can also use it for **e-greetings**.

Since there are several occasions for greeting cards, you could be making gags for all kinds of situations!

Advertising and Design Agencies

Graphic designers use **freelance cartoonists** for their projects in advertising agencies or design studios. Again, what they're looking for is a good fit with the text, in terms of illustration style. These are usually projects for the print media, as the films are contracted to film companies.

Doodle Page

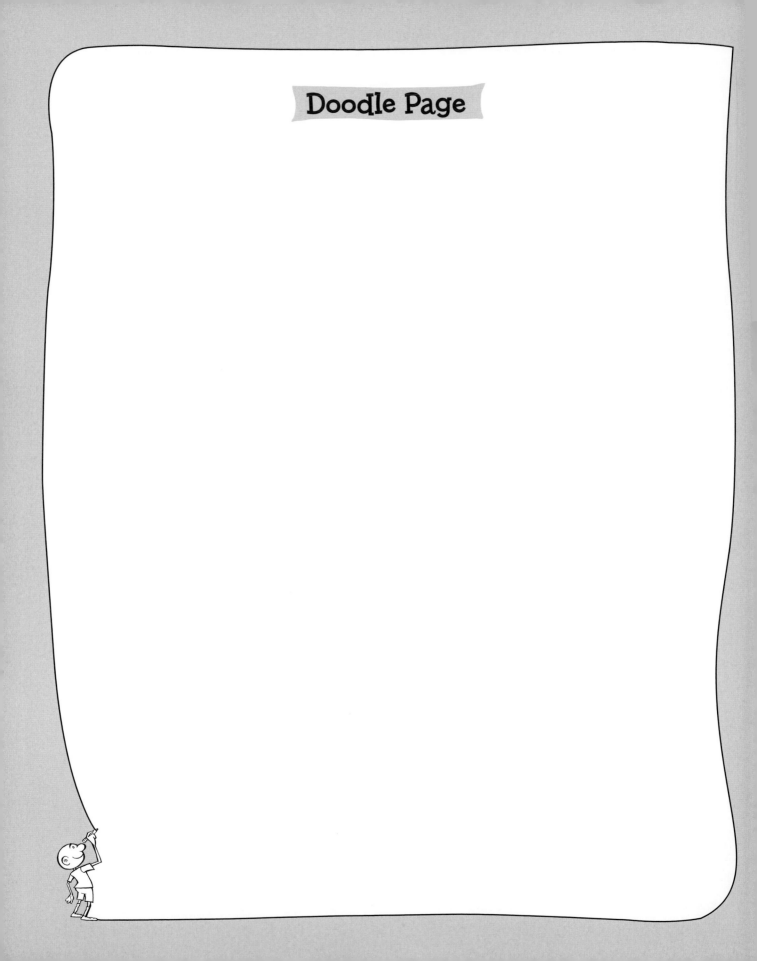

Doodle Page

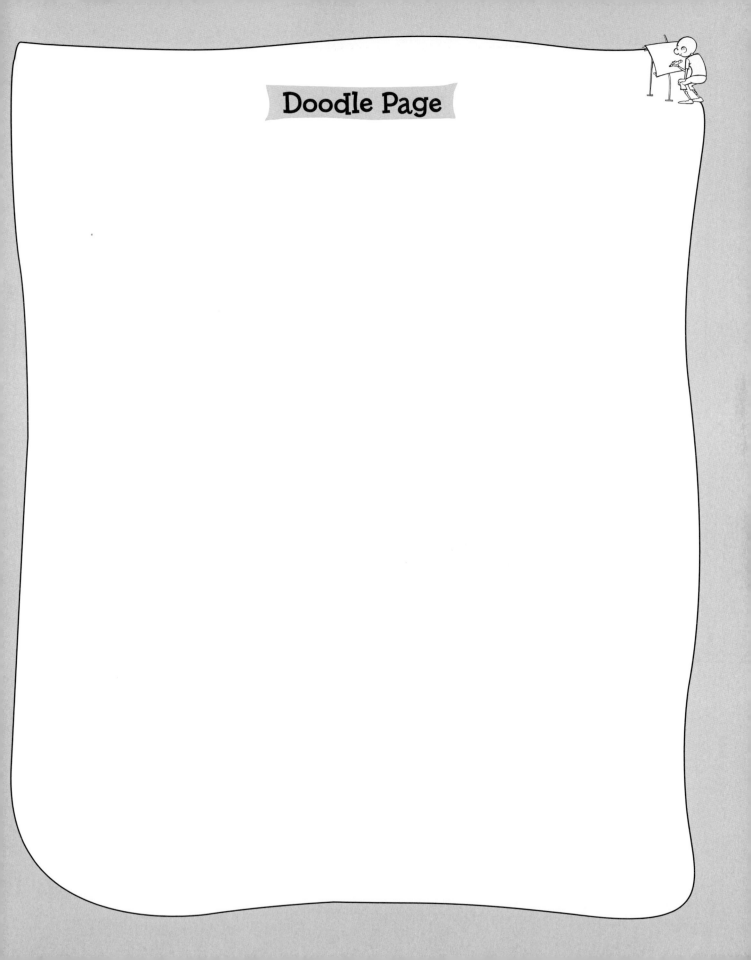

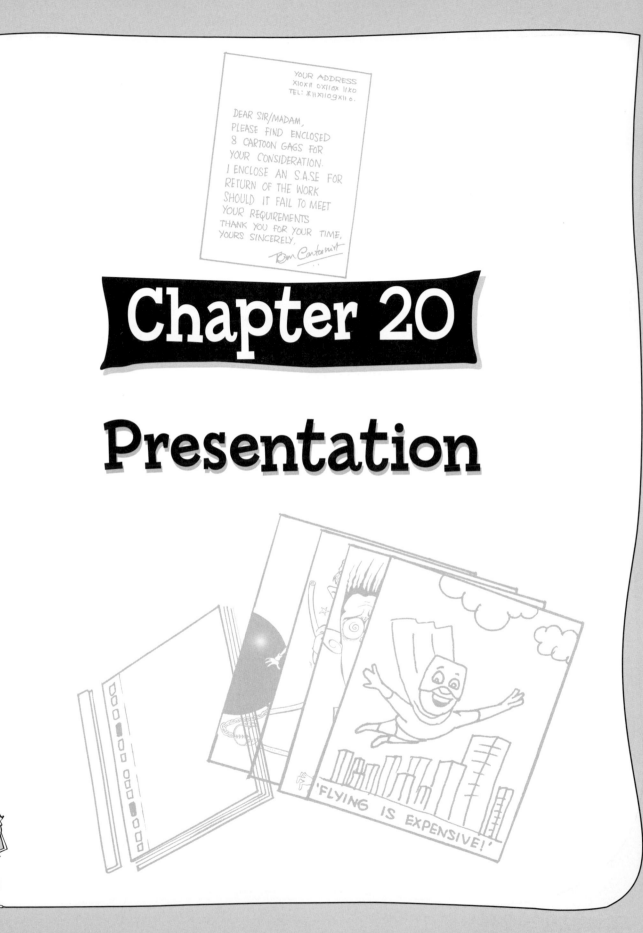

Chapter 20

Presentation

Submitting Your Work

Now that you have some creative projects ready, presenting them to potential publishers is the final step. Submit only what you think is your best work. You can submit copies of the original artwork, though you must make sure they are quality copies. Make sure to include a cover letter, stating the number and type of artwork you are submitting. Send it on a personal letterhead or include your contact details with phone number, address, and e-mail address.

YOUR ADDRESS
XIOXII OXIIOX IIXO
TEL: XIIXIIOgXII o.

DEAR SIR/MADAM,
PLEASE FIND ENCLOSED
8 CARTOON GAGS FOR
YOUR CONSIDERATION.
I ENCLOSE AN S.A.SE FOR
RETURN OF THE WORK
SHOULD IT FAIL TO MEET
YOUR REQUIREMENTS
THANK YOU FOR YOUR TIME,
YOURS SINCERELY,
Tom Cartoonist

THE EDITOR
HUMOR MAGAZINE
3, LINCO STREET
WASHINGTON D.C.

Please do not bend

Gags and caricatures should be presented as one on each page. You can send seven to ten samples. For work in black and white, you can submit clean photocopies, but for colored work you must either send the original artwork, hand-colored ink work, or a color printout of the original.

Ask yourself whether it is important for you to get your work back, or whether you would rather have a publisher file it away for future consideration. Usually, editors hold on to a gag they want to use and return the rest.

'FLYING IS EXPENSIVE!'

As for comic strips, submit about twenty-five to give the publisher an idea of the kind of humor you write and your drawing style.

Comic strips

Include some character sheets and some colored samples as well.

Character sheet

Presentation

You can have three to four daily strips on a page and about two Sunday strips on a page.

Sunday strip

Turn in your artwork in a neat folio. Stationers sell presentation files, where you can insert your artwork under a transparent sheet. You can also make a folio yourself. Attach your drawings to standard-size pages and bind them with plastic binders on the left. Avoid submitting unusually large artwork as it is difficult to file.

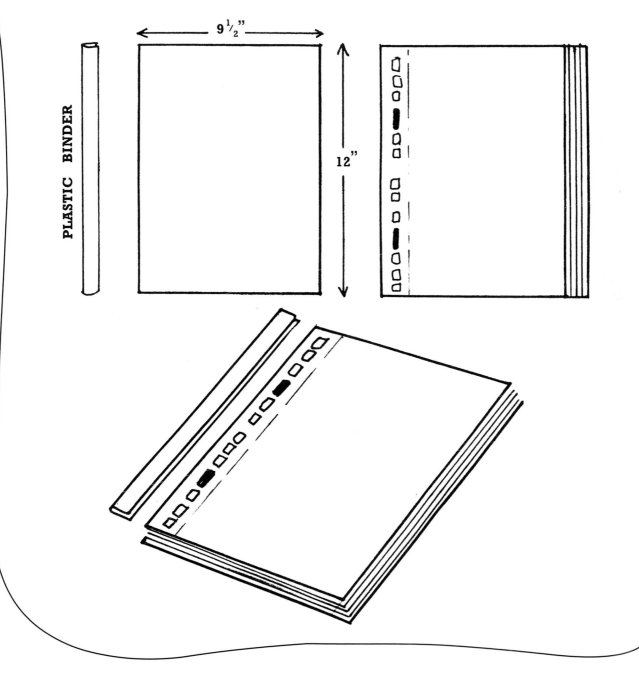

The Internet is a useful resource to find publishers who could potentially use your kind of work. Once you have their names and contact details, call their offices to find out who you can address your portfolio to. Make any other inquiries you need to at this stage.

Make a follow-up call after a week or two. They will tell you whether they like your work or not. If they don't, wait for a while and call again to ask if your work is still under consideration.

If it is not, don't worry. You can't please everyone all the time. A mark of a successful artist is taking rejection in stride and pitching to another publisher.

Keep a record of what you have submitted to which publisher. The copyright for your written and illustrated work belongs to you unless you sell it outright. For gags, you can sign your name on the artwork, but for the rest, you will need to have the copyright symbol followed by your name. You can make printouts of these and stick them on to the copies of your work.

Doodle Page

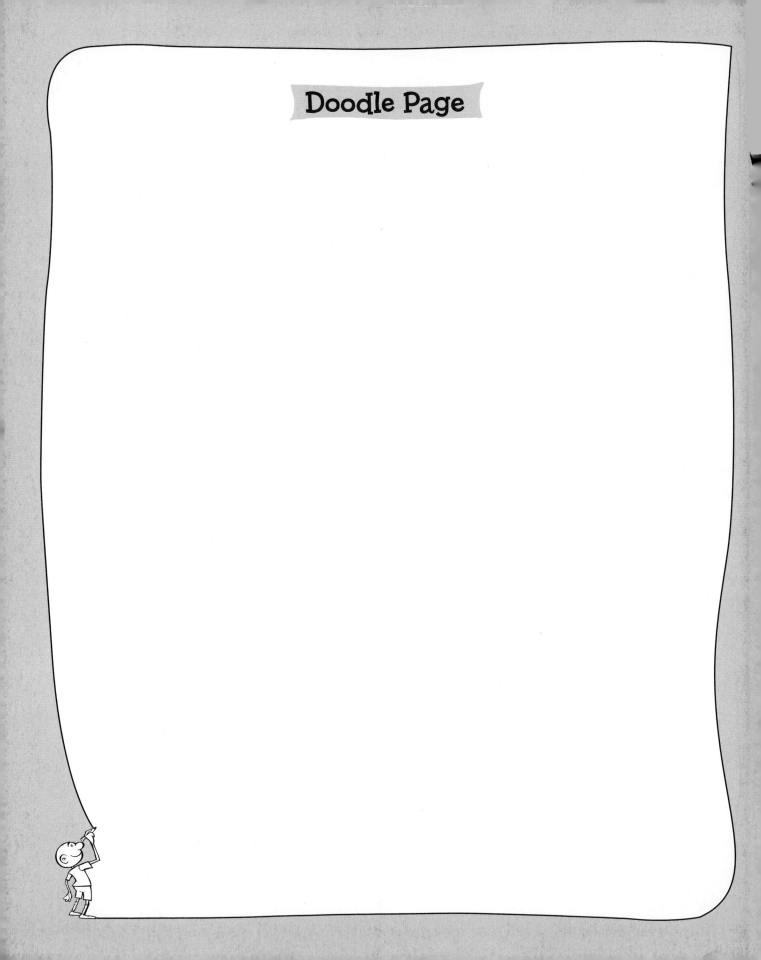